DEVELOPING AN INFORMATION LITERACY PROGRAM K–12

A How-To-Do-It Manual and CD-ROM Package

Developed by the Iowa City Community School District and edited by Mary Jo Langhorne

HOW-TO-DO-IT MANUALS FOR LIBRARIANS

NUMBER 85

NEAL-SCHUMAN PUBLISHERS, INC.
New York, London

Published by Neal-Schuman Publishers, Inc.
100 Varick Street
New York, NY 10013

The computer screen images are from the Winnebago Library System. The images are reproduced with the permission of Winnebago Software Company.®

The forms Logic Searching—Dogs and Cats are adapted from materials published by the Follett Software Company, 1391 Corporate Drive, McHenry, IL 60050.

The clipboard image in Chapter 16 is from HiWillow's *From Library Skills to Information Literacy* and is used with permission of LMCSource, PO Box 720400, San Jose, CA 95172-0400.

Library of Congress Cataloging-in-Publication Data

Developing an information literacy program K–12 : a how-to-do-it manual and cd-rom package / developed by the Iowa City Community School District and edited by Mary Jo Langhorne.
     p. cm. — (How-to-do-it manuals for libraries : # 85)
  Includes bibliographical references and index.
  ISBN 1-55570-332-1
    1. Library orientation for school children—United States.
2. Library orientation for high school students—United States.
3. Information retrieval—Study and teaching (Elementary)—United States.
4. Information retrieval—Study and teaching (Secondary)—United States.
I. Iowa City Community School District (Iowa City, Iowa) II. Langhorne, Mary Jo. III. Series: How-to-do-it manuals for libraries : no. 85.
Z711.2.d49   1998
025.5'6—dc21   98-7714
                                                        CIP

CONTENTS

PREFACE

The ability to make decisions by filtering needed information from the vast resources available today may well be *the* key skill for students who will be living and working in the twenty-first century. It is essential that students internalize a process of inquiry that includes the ability to locate, evaluate, apply, and communicate information. This ability is what defines the information-literate individual.

Library media programs are central to achieving information literacy. Newly-published national standards[1] in this area are very welcome, because they clearly articulate discrete objectives for student achievement. It is now incumbent upon local media programs to transform these standards into action by implementing successful information literacy curricula in their schools and districts. *Developing an Information Literacy Program K–12* is designed to help library media specialists achieve this goal.

This guide is not intended as a curriculum in and of itself. It is predicated on the belief that in order to be effective, the information literacy model and information seeking strategies must be taught in the context of classroom content. Such an integrated approach couples the information specialist skills of the library media specialist with the instructional and content skills of the classroom teacher to provide a collaborative approach that greatly enhances both learning and retention. Unlike other "special" areas such as art and music, library media does not have a content that can be taught in isolation. Rather, the skills, concepts, attitudes, and strategies of information acquisition, evaluation, application, and communication are best mastered by students in information problem-solving activities that are integrated with classroom curriculum.

ABOUT THIS MANUAL

Part I of this manual outlines the development of an information literacy program. All members of the school staff share the goal of enabling students to be discerning users and communicators of information. *Developing an Information Literacy Program K–12*'s first chapter outlines a process for collaboration between the teacher and library media specialist. Chapter 2 outlines a five-stage information problem-solving model. This model is a framework for teaching students the skills necessary for information literacy. When introduced at developmentally appropriate levels, it will provide a mental check-list for students whenever they need to find and use information to answer a question or solve a problem. Chapter 3 identifies and discusses the key information literacy concepts and skills that should be mastered by students as they move through a K-12 program. Assessment, both of student performance and curriculum effectiveness, must be considered at all stages of the instructional process. Chapter 4 presents tools measuring student progress as well as a matrix you can use to document your implementation of the information problem-solving model and your presentation of key concepts and skills.

Part II contains model lessons for working within the elementary program. The lessons' topics are common in elementary curricula and are intended as samples of library media/teacher collaborations that may be modified to suit your local needs. Also contained in Part II are lessons for teaching library catalog searching skills that can be used in any curriculum unit in which the library media specialist helps prepare students for an information problem-solving activity. These lessons are appropriate for use through middle school/junior high.

Part III presents sample lessons for the secondary schools. These focus heavily on teaching students the searching skills they need to use various electronic tools such as *NewsBank* or the Internet. Part IV provides ready-to-adapt templates for common instructional resources such as sample bibliographic formats, working bibliography forms, and searching aids.

ABOUT THE CD-ROM

The CD-ROM accompanying this manual contains all of the transparencies, activity sheets, forms, assessment tools, and sample documents that are described and used within the text. Special boxes throughout the manual highlight which documents are on the CD and tell you where they are located. The CD-ROM is included so that you can conveniently modify these documents to suit your own instructional needs and style. You can edit all the materials to include titles in your collection, your online catalog's searching instructions, and so forth.

HOW TO USE THE CD-ROM

The information on the CD is presented in both IBM-compatible and Macintosh formats, using Microsoft Word 6.0.1 for the Mac and Microsoft Word 7.0 for Windows.

IBM-compatible Users

1. Insert the CD-ROM in the drive and access the "C" drive (or whatever drive your CD-ROM is located in).
2. Locate the files you wish to access.
3. Click to open the files.
4. Modify them as needed.
5. Print the files.

Mac Users

1. Insert the CD-ROM in the drive.
2. Click to open the CD-ROM.
3. Locate the files you wish to access.
4. Click to open the files.
5. Modify them as needed.
6. Print the files.

ACKNOWLEDGMENTS

Developing an Information Literacy Program K-12 is the result of a collaborative study and writing process that involved teachers, administrators, parents, and library media specialists in the Iowa City Community School District who worked for two years to determine what our information literacy program should look like.

Nearly all of our district's 25 library media professionals have contributed lessons, ideas, forms, and time to this guide. This special group exhibits the very best characteristics of our profession through its commitment to helping children learn and teachers teach. Special thanks are due to Denise Rehmke for her thorough investigation of information problem-solving models and the development of the matrix and many secondary lessons; to Mary MacNeil and Dana Vernon for their work on the collaborative model and elementary lessons; to Barb Becker, Suzanne Bork, Becky Gelman, Ann Holton, and Karen Parker for the library catalog lessons; to Barb Stein and Nancy Westlake for compiling the elementary lessons; to Barb Becker, Susan Corbin Muir, Nancy

Weber, and Nancy Westlake for the elementary assessment pieces; and to Deb McAlister, Sue Richards, and Joel Shoemaker for secondary lessons and assessments. We are also indebted to the Library and Information Skills Writing Committee of the State of Montana whose excellent curriculum guide helped shape our thinking. A special note of thanks is due to Dr. Jean Donham, former coordinator of our library media program, whose continued assistance is invaluable.

All of us involved in *Developing an Information Literacy Program K–12* hope you will find it helpful in preparing your students for the twenty-first century.

ENDNOTE

1. American Association of School Librarians and Association for Educational Communications and Technology. *Information Literacy Standards for Student Learning*. Chicago: American Library Association, 1998

LIST OF FIGURES

PART I:
DEVELOPING AN INFORMATION LITERACY PROGRAM

1 INFORMATION LITERACY: A COLLABORATIVE EFFORT

The widely quoted *SCANS* [Secretary's Commission on Achieving Necessary Skills]*Report for America 2000*,[1] initiated by former Secretary of Labor Lynn Martin, lists "Information" as one of five competencies required for today's workers. It further defines four components of this information competency as follows:

- Acquires and evaluates information
- Organizes and maintains information
- Interprets and communicates information
- Uses computer to process information

These four components closely parallel the elements of the information problem-solving models developed during the past decade by Judy Pitts and Barbara Stripling; Michael Eisenberg and Robert Berkowitz; and Marjorie Pappas, Carol Kuhlthau and others. These models identify discrete information-processing tasks and suggest strategies for helping students become proficient information problem solvers.

Information literacy models describe a hands-on process where students work toward independence as information users. Beginning in the early grades, students work with information in developmentally appropriate, content-centered projects designed by the teacher and library media specialist. They learn to recognize and label where they are in the process so that over time they can step through an information problem-solving task independently. Critical thinking and evaluation skills are built in at each step of the process so that students evaluate their task, the information tools they use, the facts they find, the product they create, and the process. When students are able to do this on their own, they can be described as "information literate."

Research and best practice in the field today continue to support the principles outlined in the original *Information Power*,[2] that collaboration, flexible scheduling, and integration with content areas are critical components in the effective delivery of an information literacy curriculum. While it is the student's responsibility to internalize the skills, concepts, and processes that lead to information literacy, the classroom teacher, library media specialist, and principal work collaboratively to ensure that the student has opportunities within the context of the school's curriculum to acquire these competencies.

Collaborative planning involves the entire school in a cooperative, integrated process. Classroom teachers and the media specialist engage in collaborative planning to develop a curriculum that encourages the transfer of knowledge by effectively integrating library media center activities and resources with other learning experiences. The teacher brings to the planning process a knowledge of subject content and student needs; the media specialist contributes a broad knowledge of resources and technology. Together they share an understanding of teaching methods and a wide range of strategies. When this process of collaborative planning is employed, information literacy skills can be effectively integrated into the classroom curriculum, and the classroom content can serve as a vehicle for the instruction of the information problem-solving process. The integrated philosophy requires that an open schedule be maintained in the library media center. Collaboration and the integration of information problem-solving skills are most productive when there is flexible scheduling and when time is provided for teachers and the media specialist to plan together.[3] A collaborative program can only exist with the support of building and district administrators who believe in the importance of integration in ensuring information literacy. Administrators create an environment that is supportive of integration and hold the expectation that collaboration will occur.

Collaboration and communication between the classroom teacher and the library media specialist result in

- teaching students to transfer and apply knowledge leading to information literacy;
- cooperating and integrating across content areas;
- providing hands-on, project-based learning
- using school resources to the best possible effect;
- designing and producing instructional materials for specific learning applications;
- selecting additional materials to meet instructional needs;
- providing positive, successful learning experiences for all students;
- energizing the curriculum-planning process.

IDENTIFYING ROLES IN THE COLLABORATIVE PROCESS

The school administrator, the classroom teacher, and library media specialist all contribute to collaboration and integration. The school administrator promotes collaboration by participating in the planning and implementation of the school curriculum. S/he creates the necessary environment in the school by maintaining an expectation that there will be collaboration, developing schedules that provide time for collaboration, providing budgetary support for resources and equipment, and knowing the curriculum and suggesting possible areas for collaboration. The administrator encourages collaboration by acting as a resource person, understanding program goals throughout the building, supporting special projects, and monitoring the collaborative process.

The classroom teacher promotes collaboration by participating in the planning and implementation of the school curriculum and cooperating with the library media specialist in planning, teaching, and evaluating units that incorporate information literacy skills and concepts. The classroom teacher understands each student's learning needs and level of knowledge and is the content area expert. S/he articulates program needs and suggests resources for library collection development.

The library media specialist promotes collaboration by understanding the overall school curriculum. S/he participates in team meetings and curriculum planning for the building. The library media specialist provides instruction in accessing, evaluating, and communicating information, while the classroom teacher delivers the content area instruction. Cooperation is key to the success of this model.

The library media specialist also selects and maintains a collection of resources and services to meet the needs of students, both in curriculum support and for extending students' interests and skills beyond the traditional subject areas of the curriculum. S/he actively seeks input from teachers in developing this collection. Strong expertise in selection and use of resources is key to a successful program.

The library media specialist also plays a key role in technology integration. The library media center contains a variety of technologies for both information access and the creation and communication of information. The computer is a vital tool for students in organizing and presenting information. Other technologies, such as video, also make possible relevant, realistic vehicles for students to present the results of information searching activities. The leadership of the library media specialist helps ensure that technology is used appropriately and that it is regarded as a tool for learning in many contexts.

PLANNING FOR COLLABORATION

The Sample Collaborative Planning Guide in this section serves as a vehicle for the teacher and library media specialist to engage in discussion of the role each will play in integrated units. The guide structures the discussion of the information literacy model and how each of its components will be addressed in a learning activity.

As the teacher and library media specialist look toward a collaborative activity, it is important that a block of time be found so that they can talk face-to-face. They need a minimum of 15 minutes when they are both free from other duties. The sample planning guide facilitates the planning session and helps to make clear the division of responsibility as the unit unfolds.

As planning begins, it is essential that both the teacher and media specialist have a clear understanding of the unit's focus and goals. Writing an overview statement and rationale will help ensure that they understand clearly the purpose. It is also important to discuss prerequisite skills. Sometimes we may assume that students know how to use a particular resource or understand how a library tool is organized before beginning the unit. Defining the skills that the student will need helps to open the door for the media specialist to teach or review library skills and concepts.

A major portion of the planning time involves stepping through the information literacy model to determine which elements will be emphasized and again, where the library media specialist or teacher needs to present or reinforce concepts in the use of information or technology. This planning form also provides for the teacher and library media specialist to divide responsibilities and establish a timeline.

Determining the final product of the information literacy activity may also influence which technology skills will be taught or reinforced. While the research paper remains a valuable way for students to present some kinds of information at some levels, there are literally dozens of other products that can communicate the results of students' information searches. The list of products may be used in the collaborative planning process to suggest projects for creation and communication. Of course, the time needed for both teaching and for the researching and communication portions of the project must be carefully considered in the planning process.

The evaluation and assessment step in the planning process is when it is decided how to determine if students have learned what they were intended to learn. In Chapter 4, strategies for assessment of student work are discussed. It is important that students know at the beginning the criteria by which they will be assessed. This helps them greatly in understanding the assignment and its expectations. The old rule "If you don't know where you are going, you are likely to end up somewhere else" applies to both the problem definition and assessment portions of the information literacy process.

Once planning is completed and the library media center is scheduled, the project begins to unfold. Students may come as a large group to the media center for initial instruction on resources and strategies, or they may work in smaller groups with the teacher and the media specialist in the library and in the classroom. Often, after a few days

Sample Collaborative Planning Guide

Unit title:

Classroom teacher(s):   Curricular area:

Additional teacher(s):   Date:

Starting date: Due date:

Length of unit: Number of students:

Special equipment needs: Grade level:

Unit Overview

Rationale/Focus

Prerequisite skills

Information Literacy Model	T	MS
1. Define the Information Need		
2. Locate Information		
3. Process the Information		
4. Create and Communicate Results		
5. Assess Process and Product		
Culmination activities		

T=Teacher MS=Media specialist

Sample Completed Collaborative Planning Guide

Unit title: *Roald Dahl Author Study*

Classroom teacher(s): *D. Vernon*

Curricular area: *Language Arts*

Additional teacher(s): *M. MacNeil*

Date: *January 21*

Starting date: *February 15*

Due date: *March 5*

Length of unit: *4 weeks*

Number of students: *24*

Special equipment needs: *multiple copies of* Matilda

Grade level: *4*

Unit Overview *This project is designed to provide opportunities for students to explore the life of an author and understand how life experiences can affect one's writing.*

Rationale/Focus *An understanding of how an author's life experience reflects and influences how he/she writes.*

Prerequisite skills *Knowledge of definition of the term "author," key-word searching, author searching*

Information Literacy Model	T	MS
1. Define Information Need: *Read 3 Dahl books and draw parallels with his life; appreciate his work*		
2. Locate information: *location of biographies, fiction/everybody books, use library catalog*		
3. Process the Information: *read Dahl books and keep journal of similarities as* Boy *is read aloud*		
4. Create and Communicate: *prepare a chart showing commonalities with author's real life*		
5. Assess: *demonstrate ability to use library catalog; self- and peer evaluation of chart*		
Culmination activities: *view* Charlie and the Chocolate Factory; *invent recipe for your own chocolates*		

T=Teacher MS=Media specialist

SUGGESTIONS FOR STUDENT PROJECTS

The following list of possible student projects may be used in the collaborative planning process to suggest products for student work.

Written Projects

Research paper
I-Search paper
Book
Journal
Newspaper
Book jacket
Letter
Magazine
Word find
Crossword puzzle
Diary
Poem/Sonnet/Limerick
Brochure
Autobiography
Eulogy
Book review
Story problems
Fairy tale
Fable
Interview
Advertisement
Bibliography
Survey/Questionnaire
Recipe
Lyrics
Code
Lesson
Cookbook

Multimedia Projects

Game
Video
Movie
HyperStudio or other
  hypermedia stack

Power Point or other
  presentation
Slide-Tape
3-D display
Web pages

Visual Projects

Diagram
Collage
Model
Diorama
Map
Mobile
Sculpture
Demonstration
Game
Family tree
Flow chart
Time line
Photo album
Suitcase of artifacts
Terrarium
Blueprint
Cartoon
Flag
Mosaic
Totem pole
Machine
Pantomime
Mural
Classroom museum/Art
  gallery
Exhibition
Flip chart
Badges
Bumper stickers
Banner

Bulletin board display
Dance
Filmstrip
Slide show
Kid Pix slide show
Transparency
Graph/Table/Chart
Map collection
Mask
Photo essay
Poster
Shadow box
Greeting card
Costume
Flannel board
Timeline
Graphic
Computer program
Animation
Travelogue

Oral Projects

Debate
Radio program
Dialog
Oral report
Puppet show
Skit
Play
Panel discussion
Interview
Song
Speech
Storytelling
Commercial
Court Trial

in the library media center, it is useful to remain in the classroom to check progress and plan the next steps. One-on-one consultation between the student and teacher or library media specialist is essential as students engage in information searching and using information. This is the power of working collaboratively: the ability to divide instructional responsibilities and give more individual attention to students as they work through the process of solving complex problems.

A final, and too often neglected, step in the collaborative planning process is that of assessing the unit and the process itself. As teacher and library media specialist assess an activity or unit, the following questions should be discussed:

- Will this unit be taught again? When?
- What worked well in the unit?
- What materials were most helpful?
- What materials were not available and should perhaps be ordered if the unit is to be done again?

The *time elements* of the unit should also be discussed.

- Did materials from other sources arrive in time?
- Was the teacher's instructional time adequate?
- Did the library media specialist have enough time for instruction?
- Was the time allotted for collaborative planning adequate?
- Was there adequate time for the completion of student projects?

Taking the time to assess a completed unit using the form for Assessing a Collaborative Unit and making notes on suggested changes will prove to be a timesaver when the unit is done again.

ASSESSING THE SCHOOL CLIMATE FOR COLLABORATION

The following questions will help you assess whether the climate for collaborative planning exists in your school or district. If the answers to significant numbers of these question are negative, you will need a public relations effort for school administrators, staff, and parents.

Does the school district maintain policies that encourage the collaborative planning process?
Are all participants' roles clearly defined?

Does the school schedule allow time for collaboration?

Is there a commitment to integrated instruction?

Is there a commitment to challenging students with inquiry-based learning?

Does the process address all content areas of the curriculum?

Does the school climate encourage cooperation and lead to increased and more appropriate uses of resources?

Do the principal, teachers, and media specialists participate actively in the planning and implementation of the school curriculum?

Does the principal create the necessary environment in the school to encourage collaboration?

Does the classroom teacher

cooperate with the library media specialist in planning, teaching, and evaluating units?

contribute an understanding of students' learning needs and level of knowledge?

provide content area experience?

offer specific knowledge of the curriculum?

teach content area as agreed upon with library media specialist?

proactively articulate program needs?

Does the media specialist

create a climate in the media program that encourages collaboration?

provide instruction in assessing, evaluating, and communicating information?

develop, with teacher input, a collection of resources and services that meets the needs of the students and curriculum?

cooperate with the teachers in planning, teaching, and evaluating?

teach an information literacy curriculum as agreed upon with teacher?

extend students' interests and skills beyond the traditional subject areas of the curriculum?

Does the collaborative process include a way to assess student learning?

Does the collaborative process improve the overall educational effectiveness for children in the school district?

Information literacy is the responsibility of everyone in the school. Collaborative planning and the integration of classroom content with the library media center processes provide a means to address that responsibility.

ENDNOTES

1. *What Work Requires of Schools: A SCANS* [Secretary's Commission on Achieving Necessary Skills] *Report for America 2000.* Washington, D.C.: U.S. Department of Labor, 1991.
2. American Association of School Librarians. *Information Power: Guidelines for School Library Media Programs.* Chicago: American Library Association, 1988.
3. Ann Holton and Chris Kolarik. "Information Skills and Technology." Iowa City Community School District, 1995.

To use or modify a copy of the Collaborative Planning Guide, follow these steps:

1. Open the CD-ROM and go to the Chapter 1 Folder.
2. Click to open the Folder.
3. Click on Collaborative Planning Form to open.
4. You may modify the form to suit your own needs.

To print a list of Sample Products:

1. Open the CD-ROM and go to the Chapter 1 Folder.
2. Click to open the Folder.
3. Click on Product List to open.
4. You may add or delete products to suit your needs.

To access the assessment form:

1. Open the CD-ROM and go to the Chapter 1 Folder
2. Click to open the Folder.
3. Click Unit Assessment Form to open.

ASSESSING A COLLABORATIVE UNIT

Unit title _____   Date _____

Assessment is an essential component of an effective school. Library media specialists and teachers can assess a collaborative unit by answering the following questions:

Will this unit be taught again? When?

What worked well in the unit?

What materials were most helpful?

What materials were not available?

Assess *time elements* of the unit:

- materials acquisition:

- instructional time of teacher:

- instructional time of library media specialist:

- collaborative planning time:

Notes:

2 A FIVE-STAGE INFORMATION LITERACY MODEL

The information competencies of the SCANS report, cited in Chapter 1, have become recurring themes in education. Critical thinking, information retrieval skills, problem solving, strategic thinking, and communication skills are cited repeatedly in many contexts as key qualities for the "knowledge workers" of the future. The new Information Literacy Standards from the American Association of School Librarians and the Association for Educational Communications and Technology (AASL/AECT) describe the information-literate individual as one who can access, evaluate, and communicate information effectively.[1] Technology is a powerful tool for helping students become information literate. However, technology by itself will not bring about positive change in education if it is used simply to do all of the old things faster and in a more "entertaining" way. Technology will change education and advance information literacy only when it is recognized as a tool to foster inquiry and a means to engage students in real-world problem-solving.

"Helping students learn to identify problems of all kinds and develop strategies for solving them successfully is one of our primary educational goals," write Linda Knapp and Allen Glen, authors of *Restructuring School with Technology*.[2] Library media centers and librarians play a key role in helping students solve information problems because they are the people who understand information best—where to find it, how to use it, how to evaluate it and, increasingly, how to use new tools to communicate results once the information problem is solved.

Many of us learned a problem-solving model in secondary school science classes. This model outlined an orderly process of defining a hypothesis and then performing some sort of experiment or research to validate our hypothesis or answer our question. Along the way we recorded our observations and used those observations for drawing conclusions to be presented to the class or teacher. In recent years, many leaders in the library media field have worked with a similar idea to develop information problem-solving or information literacy models. Each of these models is based upon the idea that students need to internalize a process upon which they can call whenever they have an information need. Such a logical, standard process leads students to understand specifically what information is needed, how and where to find that information, how to process and present it, and how to evaluate the process they have engaged in as well as the product they have created. There can be little doubt that the ability to use such a process will be vital in dealing with the vast amounts of information bombarding the residents of the twenty-first century.

Most information problem-solving models describe a fairly similar set of stages that individuals pass through as they engage in the research process. Models developed by Dr. Carol Kuhlthau[3] and by Barbara Stripling and the late Dr. Judy Pitts[4] place heavy emphasis on "presearching," that is, developing a clear focus for one's topic and planning the research carefully before starting to locate information. Perhaps the best-known of the information problem-solving models is the "Big6," developed by Michael Eisenberg and Robert Berkowitz.[5] There is a *Big6 Newsletter* and a Big6 listserv, where individuals can share lessons and their experiences in using that model.

Marjorie Pappas and Ann Tepe[6] have developed a model that illustrates the recursive nature of the research process. Clearly, solving an information problem is not typically a linear process; many things happen along the way that cause us to go back and adjust our focus or try different sources of information. The American Association of School Librarians has recently published a seven-step model for information literacy that was originally developed by the Wisconsin Educational Media Association.[7] June Gross, of the Osseo, Minnesota, area schools, has developed a five-stage model that focuses on learner outcomes for each step in the process.[8] Library media specialists may wish to examine these and other available models before deciding which works best for their particular setting

The five-stage model in this chapter, and the lessons in this guide outline a streamlined process for helping students solve information problems. In stage one, **define the information need**, attention is focused on gaining a clear understanding of the problem to be solved. All too often students come to the library media center with a fuzzy understanding of exactly what it is they are being asked to do. Collaboration between the library media specialist and teacher in planning the assignment can help to eliminate much of this confusion. Teaching students a process for focusing their topic by asking careful questions, exploring subtopics, and using other strategies will save time and improve the quality of the product. This is the time to think about what the product of this information problem-solving activity will be. It is important to consider this step early, because it has an impact on the kind of information that must be found. If a multimedia project is the goal, the student must be sure to look for sound and visuals when locating information. Often the teacher determines the end product in advance, and students must consider those requirements as they begin researching.

Five-Stage Information Literacy Model

Define the Information Need	Locate Information	Process the Information	Create and Communicate Results	Assess Process and Product
Focus topic • Develop search statement • Decide what information is needed • Identify key words Determine format for the end product	Develop a research plan Determine best sources Locate sources Find information within sources	Interpret the information Evaluate usefulness of the information Extract and record information Draw conclusions	Organize information from all sources Create a product to communicate the information Cite sources used Present/perform/share	Evaluate the research process Evaluate the quality of the product

Library media specialists have always been skilled in helping **locate information**—the second stage of the information literacy model. The modern library media center contains abundant sources, including traditional tools such as books, video, and other nonprint materials as well as a wealth of electronic tools—from indexes to full-text newspaper and magazine sources to the Internet. In this stage of locating information it is important to help students understand which source is best for a given information need. How many of us have seen a student jump onto the Internet to find a map when the trusty atlas stand is located just a step away? It is important to stress that understanding the appropriateness of a tool is a critical evaluation step in locating information. Many other types of evaluation are used at this stage in the process, including judging relevance, suitability, and reliability of the author (see Chapter 3).

Processing information, once found, is often a difficult stage for students. The more clearly focused their topics are, the easier this stage should be. Students must find an efficient way to record information that they have judged to be relevant to their search. Ethical use of information is stressed at this stage. Students compare information from different sources, look for trends and patterns, and begin to draw conclusions. The library media specialist must continue to work closely with them during this stage. We cannot assume that our job has ended once the information has been found. Ideally, both the library media specialist and the teacher will work one-on-one with individuals, helping them to think critically about information as they complete this difficult step in the process.

Create and communicate results encompasses the important stage of synthesis. The student will organize the information gathered into a logical sequence and create a product. Increasingly library media specialists remain involved in this stage of the project, introducing new tools, such as electronic presentation software, which may be used as products. HyperStudio, Power Point or other presentation software may be introduced. Proper citation skills are often taught by the library media specialist at this stage as well.

The final step–**Assessing the process and product**—provides an opportunity for the student, teacher, and media specialist to reflect upon what went well and what could be improved in both the process and the product of the information problem-solving activity. Reflection and self-evaluation are important components of this step. Rubrics and other assessment tools that may be used at this stage are located in Chapter 4.

An expanded form of the five-step information literacy model follows. It is also incorporated into the K-12 curriculum matrix in Chapter 4 to provide a means to document use of the model with students.

ENDNOTES

1. American Association of School Librarians and Association for Educational Communications and Technology. *Information Literacy Standards for Student Learning.* Chicago: American Library Association, 1998.
2. Linda Roehrig Knapp and Allen D. Glenn. *Restructuring Schools with Technology.* Boston: Allyn and Bacon, 1996.
3. Carol Kuhlthau. *Teaching the Library Research Process.* New York: Center for Applied Research in Education, 1985.
4. Barbara Stripling and Judy M. Pitts. *Brainstorms and Blueprints: Teaching Library Research As a Thinking Process.* Englewood, Colo.: Libraries Unlimited, 1988.
5. Michael B. Eisenberg and Robert E. Berkowitz. *Information Problem-Solving: The Big Six Skills Approach to Library and Information Skills Instruction.* Norwood, N.J.: Ablex, 1990.
6. Marjorie Pappas and Anne Tepe. *Teaching Electronic Information Skills: A Resource Guide for Grades K-5.* McHenry, Ill.: Follett Software, 1995.
7. "Information Literacy: A Position Statement on Information Problem Solving." Chicago: American Association of School Librarians, 1994.
8. June Gross. "K-12 Media Program Outcomes." Osseo, Minn., Area Schools, 1995.

The information literacy model is presented in several formats on the CD-ROM, including the basic model, templates for bookmarks and posters, and the expanded model. To open these files:

1. Open the CD-ROM and go to the Chapter 2 Folder.
2. Click to open the Folder.
3. Scroll to the item you wish to view or print.
4. Click to open.

Expanded Five-Stage Information Literacy Model

STAGE 1: DEFINE THE INFORMATION NEED

Determining the purpose and need for the information.

Task	Strategy/Concept
✔ Focus topic • Develop search statement Decide what information is needed • Formulate questions to guide research. • Relate questions to prior knowledge. • Identify key words and names. • Develop statement of purpose (thesis).	• Presearch planning sheet, Chapters 5 and 27 • Webbing, clustering, outlining, semantic mapping • Brainstorming • Search strategy worksheet, Chapter 27
✔ Determine the format for the end product. • Consider appropriate, effective, feasible formats. • Consider audience. • Consider availability and suitability of production resources. • Consider specific requirements of instructor	• Suggestions for Student Projects Chapter 1

STAGE 2: LOCATE INFORMATION

Locating information sources and information within sources using various tools.

Task	Strategy/Concept

✔ Develop a research plan.
 	
    • Complete Research Guide.
 	
    • Determine project timeline.
	
	• Search Strategy Worksheet and Research Guide, Chapter 27.
	
	• Key words, Boolean connectors
	
	• Search statement
	
	• Identify potential sources

✔ Determine best sources
 	
    • Examine possible sources, assessing which are most relevant
 	
    • Assess suitability of potential resources considering the time frame, scope, and range of the topic.
 	
    • Assess suitability of potential resources considering their availability.
	
	• Brainstorming
	
	• Prepared bibliographies, pathfinders, or research guide; see Chapters 27–28.

Task	Strategy/Concept
✔ Locate sources.	
• Use print and electronic reference tools.	• Index or search/find features of each reference tool
• Use print and electronic information access tools including: library catalogs (building, district, and off-site) periodical indexes (*Readers' Guide, Magazine Article Summaries, NewsBank, SIRS*). *Internet (World Wide Web, Scholastic, National Geographic KidsNet)*	• Search/find features of each tool • Key words • Boolean • Truncation
• Use community resources (individual and agency)	
✔ Find information within sources.	
• Use print and electronic search features.	• Index (page, chapters, frames, tracks) • Table of contents • Chapter or section headings • Navigational features (guide words, search and find commands, cross references, bookmarks)

• Scan, screen, and select appropriate resources.	

• Apply filtering criteria such as
     - currency
     - point of view or bias
     - reliability/accuracy
     - primary/secondary source
     - availability
     - scope or depth
     - level of sophistication
      (suitability)
     - appropriateness (ethical)
	• Evaluation of sources
	• Seven Quick Ways to Evaluate Information, Chapter 3.
	
	• Acceptable use (Internet)

• Prepare working bibliography/research log.	See Chapter 26.

STAGE 3: PROCESS THE INFORMATION

Use resources, critical thinking and recording tools to gain needed information

Task	Strategy/Concept
✔ Interpret the information within a source.	
• Read, view, listen to the information.	• Use well-known strategies such as SQ3R, skimming, and scanning • Use thinking skills to appraise, draw inferences, integrate with previous knowledge
✔ Evaluate the relevance and usefulness of the information.	
• Use critical reading, viewing, listening techniques.	• Seven Quick Ways to Evaluate Information, Chapter 3 • Acceptable Use (Internet)

✔ Extract and record relevant information.	<ul><li>notetaking</li><li>photocopying/highlighting</li><li>drawing</li><li>collecting artifacts</li><li>video/audio recording</li><li>scanning</li><li>downloading</li></ul>
• Observe copyright laws.	• Ethical use of information; fair use guidelines
✔ Draw conclusions • Identify/infer relationships.	<ul><li>trends and patterns</li><li>similarities and differences</li><li>compare and contrast</li><li>cause and effect</li><li>classification</li></ul>

STAGE 4: CREATE AND COMMUNICATE RESULTS

Synthesizing information drawn from a range of resources.

Task	Strategy/Concept
✔ Organize information from all sources.	• Synthesize information • recognize logical sequence • recognize subtopics and relationships • outline • storyboard
✔ Create a product to communicate the information.	• Consider audience • Create product • Proofread/practice
✔ Cite all sources used (bibliography).	• Bibliography Style Sheet; See Chapter 28.
✔ Present/perform/share.	

STAGE 5: ASSESS PROCESS AND PRODUCT

Judging the product and process based on a set of criteria.

Task	Strategy/Concept
✔ Evaluate the research process.	• Self-reflect • Seek external feedback (peers, teachers, parents) • Adjust strategies for future research
✔ Evaluate the product.	• Self-reflect • See assessment tools, Chapter 4 • Seek external feedback (peers, teachers, parents) • Adjust strategies for future research

Information Literacy Model

Define the Information Need
- What is the information problem to be solved?
- What types of information will be needed?
- What format is best for the end product?

Locate Information
- What are all of the sources that might be used?
- Where are the sources located?
- Which are the most relevant sources?
- Where is the information within each source?

Process the Information
- What information does the source provide?
- What portion of the information is the most useful?
- How will you record the relevant information?
- How does the information relate to other data?

Create and Communicate Results
- Organize information from all of the sources.
- Create a product to communicate the information.
- Cite all sources used.
- Present/perform/share.

Assess Process and Product
- Was the information problem solved?
- Was the process efficient and effective?
- What would you do differently next time?

Information Literacy Model

Define the Information Need
- What is the information problem to be solved?
- What types of information will be needed?
- What format is best for the end product?

Locate Information
- What are all of the sources that might be used?
- Where are the sources located?
- Which are the most relevant sources?
- Where is the information within each source?

Process the Information
- What information does the source provide?
- What portion of the information is the most useful?
- How will you record the relevant information?
- How does the information relate to other data?

Create and Communicate Results
- Organize information from all of the sources.
- Create a product to communicate the information.
- Cite all sources used.
- Present/perform/share.

Assess Process and Product
- Was the information problem solved?
- Was the process efficient and effective?
- What would you do differently next time?

Information Literacy Model

Define the Information Need
- What is the information problem to be solved?
- What types of information will be needed?
- What format is best for the end product?

Locate Information
- What are all of the sources that might be used?
- Where are the sources located?
- Which are the most relevant sources?
- Where is the information within each source?

Process the Information
- What information does the source provide?
- What portion of the information is the most useful?
- How will you record the relevant information?
- How does the information relate to other data?

Create and Communicate Results
- Organize information from all of the sources.
- Create a product to communicate the information.
- Cite all sources used.
- Present/perform/share.

Assess Process and Product
- Was the information problem solved?
- Was the process efficient and effective?
- What would you do differently next time?

Information Literacy Model

Define the Information Need
- What is the information problem to be solved?
- What types of information will be needed?
- What format is best for the end product?

Locate Information
- What are all of the sources that might be used?
- Where are the sources located?
- Which are the most relevant sources?
- Where is the information within each source?

Process the Information
- What information does the source provide?
- What portion of the information is the most useful?
- How will you record the relevant information?
- How does the information relate to other data?

Create and Communicate Results
- Organize information from all of the sources.
- Create a product to communicate the information.
- Cite all sources used.
- Present/perform/share.

Assess Process and Product
- Was the information problem solved?
- Was the process efficient and effective?
- What would you do differently next time?

Information Literacy Model

Define the Information Need
- What is the information problem to be solved?
- What types of information will be needed?
- What format is best for the end product?

Locate Information
- What are all of the sources that might be used?
- Where are the sources located?
- Which are the most relevant sources?
- Where is the information within each source?

Process the Information
- What information does the source provide?
- What portion of the information is the most useful?
- How will you record the relevant information?
- How does the information relate to other data?

Create and Communicate Results
- Organize information from all of the sources.
- Create a product to communicate the information.
- Cite all sources used.
- Present/perform/share.

Assess Process and Product
- Was the information problem solved?
- Was the process efficient and effective?
- What would you do differently next time?

Five-Stage Information Literacy Model

Define the Information Need

✔ What is the information problem to be solved?
✔ What types of information will be needed?
✔ What format is best for the end product?

Locate Information

✔ What are all of the sources that might be used?
✔ Which sources will be most useful?
✔ Where are the sources located?
✔ Which are the most relevant sources?
✔ Where is the information within each source?

Process the Information

✔ What information does the source provide?
✔ What portions of the information is the most useful?
✔ How will you record the relevant information?
✔ How does the information relate to other data?

Create and Communicate Results

✔ Organize information from all of the sources.
✔ Create a product to communicate the information.
✔ Cite all sources used.
✔ Present/perform/share.

Assess Process and Product

✔ Was the information problem solved?
✔ Was the process efficient and effective?
✔ What would you do differently next time?

3 KEY INFORMATION LITERACY CONCEPTS AND SKILLS

The K-12 information literacy curriculum is a continuum along which skills and various tools and technologies are introduced, expanded, reviewed through additional practice, and refined with increasing levels of complexity and sophistication as the learner matures. This ongoing process incorporates direct instruction coupled with new opportunities for application to help the student achieve greater competence and independence.

The elementary school curriculum teaches students the basic skills needed to use information tools and resources. The curriculum emphasizes library organization and use of standard library materials such as books, encyclopedias, and almanacs to locate information. The use of the electronic library catalog and electronic encyclopedias and the skills necessary to use such information technologies are also areas of concentration. Use of the Internet may be addressed in structured ways such as through the use of bookmarks (see page XX). Students also receive instruction in basic computer operation as a prerequisite to using electronic tools and creating projects using technology.

The junior high/middle school curriculum builds upon the foundation laid by the elementary curriculum. The introduction of skills and exposure to technologies that began at the elementary level are more fully developed in the middle grades. Instruction is provided in the use of additional information access tools, reference sources, and technologies that are more appropriate for older students, such as an electronic index to periodicals, full-text sources (online or CD-ROM), and more extensive use of the Internet.

At the high school level, students receive further instruction in more specialized print and electronic resources, developing an understanding of the scope and depth of these sources and tools and when and how to use each effectively. Students are taught strategies and techniques to become discriminating information consumers, able to navigate through vast amounts of information, screening and selecting that which is most relevant and appropriate to their needs.

The role of technology in the information literacy curriculum is increasingly vital. Students arrive at the secondary schools with a sound introduction to many basic technologies for information access and production. Technology is seldom the object of a lesson, but rather a tool. Giving students relevant, appropriate opportunities to use real-world technologies for information access and production is a fundamental objective.

To maximize its effectiveness, instruction in information literacy is meaningfully integrated into the overall school curriculum through the purposeful collaboration between the classroom teacher and the media specialist. Every effort is made to teach skills in context rather than in isolation.

The information literacy curriculum's goal is that students become complex thinkers: proficient in the location and use of expanding information sources and tools, as well as creative and sophisticated in the communication of newly acquired knowledge. While the information literacy model outlines the process students engage in as they solve information problems, there are certain distinct proficiencies that students must gain if they are to be effective users of libraries and information. The key concepts and skills that follow define the basics that students must master at each level of their school experience. In most cases, these skills will be woven into information problem-solving activities. For example, as students engage in their earliest research activities, location of books by call number will be taught as a component of the activity, as in the Roald Dahl collaborative activity described in Chapter 1. As older students are asked to prepare a multimedia presentation, use of HyperStudio may be taught. This is not a list of skills to be taught in isolation, but rather an attempt to isolate skills and concepts for which the library media specialist takes responsibility. This list is not all-inclusive, and it must remain fluid to reflect the change that is a constant in our lives.

BASIC INFORMATION CONCEPTS AND SKILLS IN GRADES K–6

CONCEPT: LIBRARY ORIENTATION

Goal: Students to become familiar with using library materials and working in the library media center.

Skills
1. Listen attentively
2. Take part in discussions
3. Check out and return books responsibly

4. Understand the role of the library as a place to find materials for enjoyment and information
5. Use the media center and computer facilities productively, responsibly, and independently
6. Practice proper care and handling of print and nonprint media and equipment
7. Work independently on a project
8. Work cooperatively on a project

CONCEPT: COMPUTER SKILLS

Goal: Students develop skills in the use of a computer so that it may be used as a tool for locating and communicating information.

Skills:

1. Use the mouse to point, click, and drag
2. Understand computer skills and concepts:
   a. Quit/Exit
   b. Save to a disk
   c. Eject a disk
   d. Highlight
   e. Print
   f. Manipulate windows
   g. Pull-down/pop-up menus
   h. Tear-off menus
   i. Recognize the still-searching icon
3. Develop keyboarding skills
4. Use a word-processing program
   a. Create a document
   b. Spell check a document
5. Create a multimedia presentation

KEY CONCEPTS AND SKILLS IN GRADES K-3

CONCEPT: BASIC INFORMATION SKILLS

Goal: Students will develop an understanding of how libraries and information are organized.

Skills:

1. Understand the organizational pattern of library
2. Differentiate between fiction and nonfiction
3. Recognize call numbers and begin to understand the grouping of materials by call number
4. Begin to locate materials by call number
5. Identify the parts of a book and understand their functions:
   a. Author
   b. Title
   c. Title page
   d. Illustrator
   e. Publisher
   f. Copyright date
   g. Index
   h. Table of contents
   i. Glossary

CONCEPT: RESEARCH

Goal: Students will begin to use library sources and tools to find information.

Skills:

1. Explain an information need
2. Understand the concept of key words
3. Formulate a question about a topic
4. Begin to understand that information can be found in a variety of sources and recognize the unique features of each (e.g., dictionary, encyclopedia, atlas)
5. Begin to use table of contents and index
6. Begin to use the automated catalog
7. Begin to use electronic sources of information
8. Begin to determine possible resources and select the most appropriate
9. Understand that the needed information may be a small part of the book or source
10. Begin to understand visual literacy clues (for example., illustrations and captions, photographs, charts, tables, maps)

CONCEPT: PRODUCTION

Goal: Students will create age-appropriate projects to present information.

Skills:

1. Present information in a new form
2. Recognize the need for citing sources and begin to cite sources in a simplified manner
3. Assess both the process and the product

KEY CONCEPTS AND SKILLS IN GRADES 4–6

CONCEPT: RESEARCH

Goal: Students will develop their skills in using library sources and tools to satisfy an information need. They will become increasingly competent and independent in their use of library tools and sources.

Skills

1. Restate an assignment
2. Develop questions and identify key words about a specific topic
3. Understand that information is available in many formats
4. Generate a list of possible resources and determine which are useful
5. Make a usable presearch plan
6. Demonstrate skill in using an electronic catalog and other information sources
   a. Search by title, author, and key word
   b. Recognize information on an itemized list
   c. Use the search, sort, and select procedures
   d. Use a presearch strategy
   e. Print a list of selected resources
   f. Begin using Boolean operators to complete logic searches
7. Find information within sources using key words to access information in the following types of sources and understand important attributes of each type of source.
   a. Nonfiction books and the function of
      i. Arrangement/pagination
      ii. Table of contents and index
   b. Encyclopedias (print and electronic) and the use of
      i. Index
      ii. Cross references

        iii. Visual aids
        iv. Main headings and subheadings
        v. Guide words (print)
        vi. Hyperlinks (electronic)
        vii. Outline
    c. Almanacs
    d. Biographical and geographical sources
    e. Internet/World Wide Web, including the use of
        i. Bookmarks
        ii. Search engines

8. Identify and extract relevant information in print and electronic resources
9. Use paraphrasing, note taking, and other strategies to record the results of their information searches
10. Understand the need for the citation of sources of information (copyright)

CONCEPT: PRODUCTION

Goal: Students will begin to function as creators of knowledge by completing projects that communicate the results of their information searching. These projects will take a variety of forms.

Skills:
1. Organize the results of an information search
2. Present the results of an information search in a new form
3. Communicate the results of an information search in a format appropriate for the content
4. Proofread and edit the products
5. Cite information sources (compile a bibliography)
6. Evaluate the projects
7. Evaluate the search process

KEY CONCEPTS AND SKILLS IN JUNIOR HIGH/MIDDLE SCHOOL

CONCEPT: LIBRARY ORIENTATION

Goal: Students will become familiar with the library program.

Skills:
1. Understand the goals, purposes, and the services offered
2. Increase their awareness of available resources
3. Observe the policies and protocols

CONCEPT: RESEARCH

Goal: Students will become more effective and efficient information consumers. They will become increasingly independent in their ability to identify and satisfy information needs. Technologies will be used as tools to facilitate the research process.

Skills:
1. Articulate an information need or restate an assignment
2. Understand the scope and depth of a wide variety of available resources
3. Predict which resources will be the most useful
4. Identify useful key words
5. Identify Boolean connectors and understand their effects on search results
6. Be aware of truncation as a method of search expansion
7. Construct an effective search statement
8. Use print and electronic reference sources competently and independently
   a. General encyclopedias
   b. Almanacs
   c. Atlases
   d. Biographical references
   e. Geographical references
   f. Historical references
   g. Scientific references
9. Use print and electronic information access tools competently and independently

      a. Library catalogs (building, district)

      b. *Magazine Article Summaries (MAS)* or other electronic magazine tool

      c. Internet/World Wide Web, including Search engines

10. Find information within sources using unique search and navigational features
11. Select appropriate resources by applying filtering criteria such as availability, currency, suitability, relevance, scope, or depth
12. Use technology features to extract information (for example, copy/paste, download) from electronic sources (library network, CD-ROM, Internet)
13. Use information ethically

      a. Observe copyright guidelines

      b. Understand the concept of plagiarism and cite sources properly

      c. Comply with Internet guidelines and protocols as defined by the school or school district

CONCEPT: PRODUCTION

Goal: Students will create products that communicate their knowledge. They will make use of different technologies as tools to facilitate the production of these products.

Skills:

1. Use a graphic organizer to synthesize information from multiple sources (outlining, storyboarding)
2. Create presentation visuals using software such as HyperStudio, Power Point
3. Create multimedia products using software such as HyperStudio, Photoshop
4. Scan images
5. Create a video
6. Prepare a bibliography

KEY CONCEPTS AND SKILLS IN HIGH SCHOOL

CONCEPT: LIBRARY ORIENTATION

Goal: Students will become familiar with the library program.

Skills:
1. Understand goals and purposes
2. Know the services offered
3. Know the resources that are available
4. Observe the policies and protocols

CONCEPT: RESEARCH

Goal: Students will become discriminating information consumers, able to identify and satisfy information needs independently. They will continue to use technologies as tools to facilitate the research process.

Skills:
1. Know resources that are more advanced and sophisticated—content, scope, and depth
2. Determine when to use various resources
3. Identify key words, truncation, and Boolean connectors to create search statements
4. Use the print and electronic resources listed below competently and independently
    a. Biographical references
    b. Geographical references
    c. Historical references
    d. Scientific references
    e. Literary references
    f. Statistical references
    g. Library catalogs (building, district, public library, and university library)
    h. *Magazine Article Summaries (MAS)* or other electronic magazine source
    i. *NewsBank* or other full-text sources
    j. *Social Issues Resources Series (SIRS)*
    k. *Granger's World of Poetry* (Poetry indexes)
    l. Internet/World Wide Web

5. Navigate within resources using cross references, bibliographies, bookmarks, and search/find commands
6. Apply filtering criteria to screen display and select appropriate resources to generate a feasible, comprehensive working bibliography
7. Use technology features to extract information (for example, copy/paste, download) from electronic sources (library network, CD-ROM, Internet)
8. Observe copyright guidelines
9. Observe Internet guidelines and protocols as defined by the school or school district.

CONCEPT: PRODUCTION

Goal: Students will create products relevant to the real world that communicate their findings in appropriate ways. Technologies will be used as tools to facilitate the production.

Skills:
1. Use a graphic organizer to synthesize information (outlining, storyboarding)
2. Create presentational visuals using software (PowerPoint, HyperStudio, Persuasion)
3. Create a multimedia product using software (HyperStudio, Photoshop)
4. Create a video

To access these key concepts on CD-ROM so they may be adapted to local needs:

1. Open the CD-ROM and go to the Chapter 3 Folder.
2. Click to open Folder.
3. Click on File to open.

EVALUATING INFORMATION

The information-literate individual must be able to discriminate from among the abundant resources available those that truly address a given information need. Having found appropriate sources, a student must be able to distinguish useful information from propaganda, opinion, and that which is simply irrelevant.

Goal: Students will develop critical information processing skills and learn to employ the seven basic evaluation skills readily in any information problem-solving situation.

Skills:

1. Judge the **appropriateness** of a source.

   This is the initial step in evaluation and a critical component of information literacy. This is the question of where to look for what kind of information. There is a tendency these days to jump first to the Internet for almost any type of information. While the Internet is certainly an increasingly powerful information tool, there are frequent occasions when a more traditional source, such as an almanac, is more efficient. This judgment is made at the beginning of the searching activity as a step in locating information.

   Students must learn to pose questions such as these:

   a. If I want general information, is an encyclopedia or a magazine a better choice?
   b. If I want the most current information, is a magazine article or the Internet more appropriate?
   c. If I want the most current information, is a book or a magazine article more appropriate?
   d. If I want maps, should I use the CD-ROM encyclopedia or an atlas?

2. Use **availability** as a strategy when locating information.

   With the wealth of information access tools available, including the Internet, the catalogs of public and university libraries, and resource sharing with other libraries, the range of information sources is greatly expanded. However, having a title available at the local college or even at another local school may not be a useful find if time or transportation are issues. Students must decide whether availability outside the school walls is useful.

Students should ask questions such as these:

    a. Will I be able to get to the public library during the time I have available for this project?
    b. Can I find enough information here without needing to look any further?
    c. Will my time be better spent using locally available sources or doing more searching in other places?

3. Determine quickly whether a tool is **relevant** to the information need.

This can often be done at the computer if an electronic search is being done. Key-word searching often yields "false hits," that is, references to titles that are not really related to the topic at hand. These are often found because of a misleading title or a word with more than one meaning. Students should use tables of contents, indexes, and skimming to make a determination about the relevance of a source (locating information, processing information).

Students should ask questions such as these:

    a. Does the table of contents show that a chapter or more of the book is devoted to my topic?
    b. Does the summary of the Internet site's content closely match my research need?
    c. Does the index show that a number of pages, especially ranges of pages, have information I can use?
    d. Does the abstract of the article deal directly with my subject?

4. Assess the **suitability** of relevant sources.

Students are sometimes overly impressed by "big" books—textbooks or scholarly writings. They must realize that the shortest book that deals comprehensively with the topic or a magazine or newspaper article may be more readily understood and is, therefore, more "usable" (locating information).

Students should ask questions such as these:

    a. Do I understand the title of this book?
    b. If I read one page, are there many words that I do not understand?
    c. Can I easily paraphrase what I read in the article?

5. Judge how important **currency** is to the topic and select appropriate resources.

   In some content areas, such as science, it is important to have information that is as current as possible. If one is studying the American Revolution, a book published in 1967 might be perfectly adequate while a history of the American space program published in 1967 might fail to include a few important events (locating information)!

   Students should ask questions such as these:

   a. When was this book published?
   b. Does the copyright or publication date matter in terms of my project?

6. Assess the **authority** of an author or resource.

   One of the frustrations of gathering information from the Internet is that it is often impossible to judge the author's authority. With books, magazines, and other print sources, some description of the author's background and training is usually given. As students use resources—print, electronic, and human—they must learn to question the credentials of people from whom they are accepting information (locating information).

   Sample questions to ask are

   a. What is this person's training or background in the subject?
   b. Has my teacher ever heard of this person?
   c. Is the person's or organization's identity clear from what is on their Web page?

7. Determine the **reliability** of a source.

   Often closely related to the author's authority is the idea of the reliability of the information. Does it have a strong basis in fact or is it simply the opinion of the person who is writing or speaking? Usually, reliable information will cite other reliable studies or works by different authors. Facts will be given with sources listed and can be verified by comparing with facts found in other sources (locating information, processing information). Special issues with regard to reliability arise in using the Internet, since any individual may easily publish there.

   Students should pose questions such as these:

a. Is the author's language objective and free of "loaded words" or stereotypes?
b. In the case of Internet sites, is it a commercial site, an educational site, or a site sponsored by an organization?
c. Are other sources given that can be used to verify the information?

4 ASSESSING STUDENT LEARNING

Current research supports the idea that assessment is integral to the instructional process. The purposes of assessment are many:

- to provide feedback to the student, parent, and teacher
- to promote accountability for students and teachers
- to improve instruction
- to improve performance
- to recognize accomplishment

Presenting clear assessment criteria at the beginning of an information-seeking project clarifies expectations for learners. When students are given a well-developed set of criteria for performance they are able to use those criteria as a roadmap to good performance. This philosophy places assessment in the midst of instruction, rather than treating it as a separate activity to be done after a project is completed.[1]

Assessment should be considered carefully during the instructional planning process. While in many cases the actual evaluation of the product or project will be done by the classroom teacher, the library media specialist must find ways to evaluate and document student achievement of the information literacy curriculum goals.

ASSESSMENT TOOLS

Educators have developed many different ways of assessing student performance. Today there is a strong trend away from traditional testing as a means of assessment and toward more "authentic" methods in which students are evaluated on the basis of products they create, as is the case in the business world. This type of assessment is very appropriate in the library media center, where a strong emphasis is placed on project work.

RUBRICS

Rubrics have proven to be one effective means of providing students with a "blueprint" to successful learning experiences. A rubric is a set of graduated criteria that clearly defines for student and teacher the range of acceptable and unacceptable performance. It describes "what good looks like."[2] When students are given rubrics such as the samples in this chapter at the beginning of a research project they know clearly the teacher's expectations for their performance.

Student self-evaluation is built into many of these rubrics. The last step in the information literacy model requires students to reflect on both the product of their work and the process in which they engaged. It is critical that students develop the habit of evaluating their own work objectively.

The rubrics in this chapter are samples and will need to be tailored to individual projects. They illustrate different ways of formatting and different techniques for the use of rubrics. The first three examples are designed to be used in conjunction with some of the lessons for elementary students outlined in Part II. The Multimedia Project rubrics are appropriate for use with secondary students. Parts of this set can be used independently depending upon the nature of the project.

CHECKLISTS

If a student is expected to master a skill or concept or complete a given task, a simple checklist may serve as the best means of assessment. The sample checklist (page 59) documents the attainment of basic skills in the use of the electronic catalog. Students might also complete simple checklists to record the information sources they have checked, to indicate completion of steps in the information literacy model, or to assess their own or a peer's project.

OTHER ASSESSMENT METHODS

Many other methods exist for the assessment of student work. Learning logs have been used to record progress through an information problem-solving project. Sometimes it will fit better with a teacher's evaluation system to use a simple scoring approach for the elements of a project. A sample Scorecard for Multimedia Projects is included in the forms at the end of this section. Discussions of the research process led by the media specialist can be beneficial because they encourage students to think about their work as they complete a project. Peer assessment and self-assessment are both of value in helping students recognize their accomplishments and pinpoint areas for improvement. Student multimedia projects transferred to videotape or other storage devices can become part of an electronic portfolio of assessment to show progress over time. Once on videotape, these projects can also be easily shared with parents.

COMMUNICATION WITH PARENTS

Parent involvement in a student's school activities is critical to success. The following are suggested ways to communicate with parents during the school year. Such communication serves two purposes: to provide an overview of the media program and to provide specific information about what students are doing or are able to do at a given point in the school year. By varying the ways we communicate what we do we will reach a larger number of parents, and parents will see the many aspects of our programs. This is also sound educational practice and results in the support for our library media centers, which is vital.

1. **Letters to Parents.** Letters may explain a specific collaborative project being done through the media center. A letter at the beginning of the year explaining library activities and procedures, especially for younger students, is also of value.
2. **An Invitation to Visit.** Parents are invited to come during a special event to the media center to view projects. Projects could be shown during Open House, Parents' Night, parent-teacher organization meetings, Family Technology Night, or on conference days. Multimedia projects could also be put on a video tape to be circulated.
3. **Parent-Teacher Conference Documents.** A letter to parents at elementary conference time could present an overview of the media program. A student self-assessment checklist might be included and shared at conference time.
4. **Other Ways to Communicate.** The following are a variety of ways to inform parents about the library media program.

   - Write short articles for the school newsletter about specific things happening in the media center
   - Sponsor family book talks and read-ins
   - Distribute special-events bibliographies of appropriate books, web sites, computer software, and other media
   - Prepare bulletin board displays of children's work and circulate videotaped copies of multimedia projects
   - Invite parents to attend author visits
   - Coordinate family technology nights

CURRICULUM MATRIX

To achieve the library media program mission of "enabling all students to be effective users of information and ideas,"[3] it is essential that a consistent curriculum be delivered across the district. The curriculum matrix that follows serves as a program planning and assessment tool. Based upon the information literacy model presented in Chapter 2 and the key concepts and skills in Chapter 3, the matrix outlines a sequence of skills and concepts with recommended grade levels for introduction, expansion and refinement/reinforcement. It is used to ensure that students have the appropriate prerequisite learning before new skills are introduced. The curriculum matrix included on the disk which accompanies this guide provides flexibility for media specialists to add skills and tools that may be specific to their own programs.

The curriculum matrix is also intended as a record-keeping device for library media specialists to record units and levels at which specific content is covered. Each library media specialist will identify on the curriculum matrix the specific grade level(s), unit(s), or course(s) in which various content will be taught. This will require cooperative planning with the classroom teacher to provide for the integration of information literacy skills into the classroom program. While individual schools will vary in when and where certain content is covered, the matrix will serve to document that the information literacy curriculum is being taught to all students.

ENDNOTES

1. Jean Donham van Deusen. "Assessing Information Processes: Creating Roadmaps to Success." Presentation on Tuesday, October 25, 1995, at Grant Wood Area Education Agency, Cedar Rapids, Iowa.
2. Ibid.
3. American Association of School Librarians. *Information Power: Guidelines for School Library Media Programs*. Chicago: American Library Association, 1987.

The curriculum matrix can be used to record your own progress toward information literacy goals. To open this file:

1. Open the CD-ROM and go to the Chapter 4 Folder.
2. Click to open the Folder.
3. Click on Curriculum Matrix to open.

Sample rubrics as well as the Scorecard for Multimedia and Checklist are on the CD-ROM. You will want to modify these assessment tools to suit your own projects and requirements. To access these tools:

1. Open the CD-ROM and go to the Chapter 4 Folder.
2. Click to open the Folder.
3. Scroll to the rubric you wish to use.
4. Click to open.

RUBRIC FOR KID PIX SLIDE SHOW OR HYPERSTUDIO PROJECT FOR BUTTERLY UNIT

Grade Level: 2-3

Group Members _____

Locate Information
Identifying Key Words

	Student	Teacher	
Expert			Our group was able to identify a key word for each question.
Proficient			
Apprentice			Our group was able to identify a key word for each question with help from the teacher.
Novice			Our group did not understand what a key word was.

Locate Information
Determining Possible Resources

	Student	Teacher	
Expert			Our group named both nonfiction books and reference sources specific to our topic.
Proficient			We listed books and encyclopedias as sources.
Apprentice			We listed books as sources.
Novice			We could not think of places to look for our information.

Locate Information
Finding Information within a Source

	Student	Teacher	
Expert			Our group used the index and table of contents to find information quickly.
Proficient			Our group used the table of contents and index but couldn't match it to our key word or question.
Apprentice			The teacher helped our group use the table of contents and index.
Novice			We browsed through our sources to find information.

Process the Information
Taking Notes (Understanding What Is in the Notes)

	Student	Teacher	
Expert			When we read over our notes they make sense to us.
Proficient			When we read over our notes there are only a few things we don't understand.
Apprentice			When we read over our notes there are many things we don't understand.
Novice			When we read over our notes most of information does not make sense to us.

Create and Communicate Results
Organizing Information—Using Storyboard Cards

	Student	Teacher	
Expert			Our storyboard cards were well-organized (clear text, noted pictures and sound). They made it very easy to complete our presentation.
Proficient			Our storyboard cards were complete except for one or two items. We only had to make a few choices at the computer.
Apprentice			We could read our storyboard cards but we forgot to include some information. We had to make a lot of choices at the computer.
Novice			Our storyboard cards were messy. It was hard to use them to create our presentation

Create and Communicate Results
Designing Screens

	Student	Teacher	
Expert			Screens were easy to read and view: colors, fonts, graphics work well together.
Proficient			Most screens were easy to read and view; choice of font or colors made it hard to read one or two screens.
Apprentice			Some screens were easy to read and view.
Novice			It was hard to read the information on our screens.

Create and Communicate Results
Using Titles to Organize Information in a Presentation

	Student	Teacher	
Expert			Our presentation uses titles that emphasize the main idea for each screen.
Proficient			Our titles were not completely on-target.
Apprentice			We needed more titles to guide the viewer.
Novice			We did not use titles on any of our screens.

Create and Communicate Results
Citing All Sources

	Student	Teacher	
Expert			Our group included a bibliography of all the sources we used that correctly identified author and title.
Proficient			Our group included a bibliography of some the sources we used that correctly identified author and title.
Apprentice			Our group included a bibliography of one source we used that correctly identified author and title.
Novice			We didn't list any of our sources.

RUBRIC FOR TRAVEL BROCHURE

Grade
Name _____

On Task

	Student	Teacher	
Expert			I am on task and do not distract others.
Proficient			I am on task, but sometimes I distract others.
Apprentice			I need reminders to stay on task and not distract others.
Novice			I often distract others and need to be separated from the group.

Locate Information: Using the Library Catalog to Sort and Select

	Student	Teacher	
Expert			I used the library catalog to sort and select appropriate nonfiction materials by myself.
Proficient			I used the library catalog to sort but needed help to select appropriate nonfiction materials.
Apprentice			I used the library catalog to sort but the materials I selected included both fiction and nonfiction.
Novice			I couldn't find materials on my topic in the library catalog.

Process the Information: Organizing Notes

	Student	Teacher	
Expert			My notes are organized by topic, and I have included several notes for each topic.
Proficient			My notes are organized by topic, and I have included several notes for most of the topics.
Apprentice			My notes are organized by topic, but I have only one or two notes per topic.
Novice			My notes are not organized by topic.

Process the Information: Paraphrasing

	Student	Teacher	
Expert			All of my notes are in my own words except for direct quotes.
Proficient			My notes are in meaningful phrases, but some I copied directly from my sources and did not use quotes.
Apprentice			My notes include complete sentences that I copied directly from my sources and I did not use quotes.
Novice			I copied all of my notes directly from my sources.

Create and Communicate Results: Text of Travel Brochure

	Student	Teacher	
Expert			People who read my travel brochure will call their travel agent immediately.
Proficient			People who read my travel brochure will consider visiting my state.
Apprentice			People who read my travel brochure will learn factual information about my state.
Novice			People who read my travel brochure will learn a few facts but will have a lot of questions about my state.

Create and Communicate Results: Spelling and Punctuation

	Student	Teacher	
Expert			I used spell check, and I proofread my travel brochure before printing.
Proficient			I used spell check, but I did not proofread my travel brochure before printing.
Apprentice			I forgot to use spell check, but I proofread my travel brochure before printing.
Novice			I forgot to use spell check, and did not proofread my travel brochure before printing.

Create and Communicate Results: Quality of Graphics

	Student	Teacher	
Expert			All of my graphics are eye-catching and colorful and illustrate my text.
Proficient			Most of my graphics are eye-catching and colorful and most illustrate my text.
Apprentice			My graphics attract attention but are not directly related to my text.
Novice			My graphics distract from the text because they do not relate to it.

RUBRIC FOR NOTABLE IOWANS

Grades 5/6
Final product: Magazine/ Booklet

Name: _____

Define the Information Need: Asking Questions to Guide Research

	Student	Teacher	
Expert			Some of my questions begin with "how" or "why."
Proficient			
Apprentice			Most of my questions can be answered in one or two words.
Novice			I already know the answers to all the questions I asked.

Locate Information: Selecting Sources

	Student	Teacher	
Expert			My sources had the information I needed to answer my questions, and I could find it in them.
Proficient			My sources probably had the information in them, but it was either too long or too hard or it wasn't organized so that I could find the answers I needed.
Apprentice			My sources had either too much detail or too few facts.
Novice			My sources didn't have the information I needed at all.

Locate Information:
Using Headings and Subheadings in an Information Source

	Student	Teacher	
Expert			Headings and subheadings helped me find what I needed quickly.
Proficient			
Apprentice			I looked at the headings and subheadings, but I couldn't connect them to my questions.
Novice			I did not use headings and subheadings–I browsed.

Process the Information: Notetaking–Paraphrasing

	Student	Teacher	
Expert			My notes are in my own words except for direct quotes.
Proficient			Most of my notes are in meaningful phrases, but some I copied directly from my sources and did not use quotes.
Apprentice			Most of my notes are copied directly from sources and I did not use quotes.
Novice			My notes are copied.

Process the Information: Notetaking–Relevance

	Student	Teacher	
Expert			My notes relate directly to my questions.
Proficient			My notes include information that answers my questions, but there is also information in my notes that I don't need.
Apprentice			My notes do not answer all of my questions.
Novice			My notes relate to my topic but they do not answer my questions.

Create and Communicate Results: Laying Out Pages

	Student	Teacher	
Expert			Titles, captions, and labels emphasize main ideas of the article or picture.
Proficient			Titles, captions, and labels are not meaningful or "on target."
Apprentice			The page needs more titles, captions, or labels to guide the reader.
Novice			There are no titles, captions, or labels.

Create and Communicate Results: Selecting Fonts

	Student	Teacher	
Expert			The fonts I used are an appropriate size and style to be readable.
Proficient			The fonts I used are too small or the wrong style.
Apprentice			The fonts I used were distracting. I used too many fonts.
Novice			The fonts I used make the page difficult to read.

Stage 5: Assess Process and Product

Class will construct rubric to evaluate whole magazine. Criterion for expert might be "reader would want to read/view each and every page."

RUBRIC FOR MULTIMEDIA PROJECT—SECONDARY

Assessment of Computer Skills

1. **Screen Design:**
   - Button placement consistent
   - Type contrast pleasing
   - Type style readable
   - Icons appropriate
   - Backgrounds unobtrusive
   - Graphics pleasing and clear

Expert		Clear; appealing; navigate easily
Proficient		Usable; can navigate
Apprentice		Usable but confusing; navigation not consistent
Novice		Cannot read; inconsistent

2. **Program Operation:**
   - Contains Menu or Quit button on every page
   - Buttons work as stated
   - Sound is clear
   - Special features function properly

Expert		Bug free; flows freely and consistently
Proficient		Mostly bug free; meets all requirements
Apprentice		Works but has some bugs
Novice		Does not work; inconsistent

3. **Program Design:**
   - Has title page and production credits
   - Provides appropriate branching opportunities
   - Returns to a recognizable point, e.g., menu
   - Uses logical and intuitive icons

Expert		Well designed; logical flow; clear links
Proficient		Works
Apprentice		Usable but confusing; navigation not consistent
Novice		Many dead ends; does not flow

4. **Use of Resources:**
   - Incorporates relevant pictures and graphics
   - Takes advantage of medium's capabilities

Expert		Optimal use; adds to overall design; adds to information transfer
Proficient		Acceptable use
Apprentice		Majority acceptable; missed opportunities; few links to information
Novice		No graphics or sound links to information

Assessment of Content

1. Research:
- Uses varied relevant sources
- Has notes with source documented
- Cites sources in bibliography
- Avoids plagiarism

Expert		Has more than required sources; good variety and reliable sources
Proficient		Required sources
Apprentice		Required number of sources; reliability doubtful
Novice		Has fewer than required number of sources; citations not clear

2. Subject:
- Demonstrates depth of knowledge
- Synthesizes information
- Supports facts

Expert		Clear understanding with demonstrated contextual aspects
Proficient		Some understanding of whole view demonstrated
Apprentice		Little understanding of contextual aspects
Novice		No understanding of topic demonstrated

3. Organization:
- Introduction clearly states purpose
- Thesis is clear
- Logical progression of information
- Graphics further explain or clarify text
- Conclusion clear

Expert		Logical progression; good supporting evidence; flows smoothly; cohesive
Proficient		Connections clear; somewhat jumpy; lacks clear cohesion
Apprentice		Limited connections between information
Novice		Lacking connections between information; disjointed

4. Accuracy and Cohesion:
- Text is current and factual
- Pictures correlate to text
- Sound tied to text

Expert		Text, graphics, and sound are accurate and not biased
Proficient		Accurate
Apprentice		Mostly accurate; not consistent; components not unified
Novice		Inaccurate

Assessment of Cooperative Learning

1.   Workload/Productivity
- Contributes orally in class
- Contributes with written material to the group project
- Contributes ideas to group
- Willingness to contribute

Expert		Equitable contribution
Proficient		Adequate contribution
Apprentice		Little contribution
Novice		No contribution

2.   Dependability:
- Attends class
- Meets deadlines
- Brings supplies

Expert		Always
Proficient		Usually
Apprentice		Sometimes
Novice		Never

3. Integration of Work/ Collaboration of Effort:
- No bickering or whining
- Willingness to adapt work as needed
- Revise work as needed to fit group project
- Accepts constructive comments
- Ability to tactfully provide constructive comments
- Gives positive feedback to group

Expert		Always
Proficient		Usually
Apprentice		Sometimes
Novice		Never

Assessment of Presentation

1.   Oral:
- Good eye contact
- Entire audience can hear
- Conveys confidence
- Is positive, shows enthusiasm in voice

Expert		Poised; comfortable with information; able to answer questions
Proficient		Some eye contact; able to answer most questions
Apprentice		Unable to answer questions; not at ease with topic; poor eye contact
Novice		Poorly prepared; unsure

2.   Mechanics:
- Punctuation
- Spelling
- Grammar–Basic verb tenses
- Appropriate use of language
- Supported facts

Expert		Complex sentences; correct grammar; error free
Proficient		Correct grammar; mostly error free
Apprentice		Some problems
Novice		Poor grammar and spelling

- Graphics serve a purpose
- Graphics enhance text
- Format of graphics is appropriate

Expert		Graphics help reinforce text
Proficient		Graphics not always connected to or supportive of text
Apprentice		Graphics sometimes distracting
Novice		Graphics lacking or distracting

LIBRARY CATALOG CHECKLIST

Student Names

Teacher _____ *Grade Level* _____								
Base Skills								
Defines author and title								
Recognizes/interprets call numbers								
Understands library arrangement								
Computer Skills:								
• mouse skills								
• still searching clock								
• save to disk								
• quit								
• eject a disk								
• open a file								
• scroll								
• window manipulation								
• pull down menu								
• highlight a selection								
• cut/paste								
• tear off menu								
Library Catalog Skills								
Enters key word/phrase correctly								
Searches by key word								
Searches by title								
Searches by author								
Uses search, sort, select procedures								
Recognizes information on a list screen								
Recognizes material types								
Understands use of Browse screen								
Understands terms: field, column								
Interprets copies in column								
Uses search screen commands								
Quits out of catalog								
Uses truncation/wild card for broadening searches								
Begins to understand Boolean operators								
Prints a list of selected resources								

SCORECARD FOR MULTIMEDIA PROJECTS

Total Points Possible _____ **Total Points Earned**_____

	Possible Points	Points Earned
1. Content • Project demonstrates a unified and coherent purpose • Locates and integrates appropriate information • Exhibits a high level of understanding of the topic	_____	_____
2. Design • Demonstrates careful organization • Incorporates a variety of graphics such as background art, clip art or freehand art, and icons • Creates appropriate navigational aids in consistent locations	_____	_____
3. Resources • Uses the components of multimedia such as print text, laser disc, scanned image, sound, specialized buttons, and animation appropriately	_____	_____
4. Creativity • Exhibits problem-solving ability in both form, content and technology • Selects and uses visual and text resources in an original manner	_____	_____
5. Writing Standards • Composition • Mechanics	_____	_____
6. Bibliography • Cites media and print resources appropriately • Adheres to copyrighting procedures	_____	_____
7. Presentation • Presenter enhances the knowledge or beliefs of the audience • Contributes to the content of the presentation through delivery • Engages the audience • Motivates audience by using novel, appropriate, and vivid word choice and examples • Uses technology effectively	_____	_____
8. Participation • Demonstrates the ability to follow multi-step directions • Uses time wisely	_____	_____
9. Collaboration • Demonstrates ability to work effectively in group settings • Willingly assists others in key skills	_____	_____

K-12 Curriculum Matrix

Stage One

Define the Information Need

	K	1	2	3	4	5	6	7	8	9	10	11	12	Curricular Integration
• Focus topic														
Explain information need/restate the assignment	I			E							R			
Formulate questions to guide research			I		E					R				
Focus/refine topic; develop purpose (thesis) statement				I		I				R			12	
• Determine the format for the end product														
Consider appropriate, effective formats; audience; availability and suitability of production resources				I		E				R		11		

I=Introduce   E=Expand   R=Refine/Reinforce

Stage Two

Locate Information

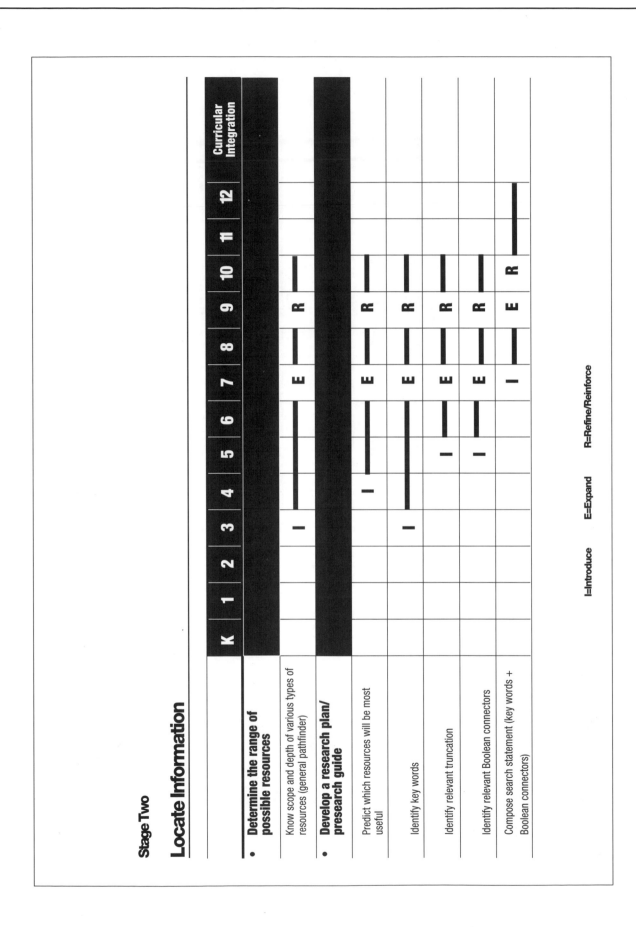

	K	1	2	3	4	5	6	7	8	9	10	11	12	Curricular Integration
• **Determine the range of possible resources**														
Know scope and depth of various types of resources (general pathfinder)				I				E		R				
• **Develop a research plan/ presearch guide**														
Predict which resources will be most useful					I			E		R				
Identify key words				I				E		R				
Identify relevant truncation						I		E		R				
Identify relevant Boolean connectors						I		E		R				
Compose search statement (key words + Boolean connectors)								I		E			R	

I=Introduce   E=Expand   R=Refine/Reinforce

	K	1	2	3	4	5	6	7	8	9	10	11	12	Curricular Integration
• Orientation to the library														
Understand library organization	I	E						E		E				
Understand resource classification or arrangement (e.g., Dewey Decimal, author)				I		E		R						
Locate resources by call number			I			E								
Identify the parts of a book	I			E				R						
• Use print and electronic reference sources														
Almanacs print / electronic				I				E						
Biographical sources					I			E						
Geographical sources						I		E		R				
Encyclopedias print / electronic						I		E		R				

I=Introduce   E=Expand   R=Refine/Reinforce

	K	1	2	3	4	5	6	7	8	9	10	11	12	Curricular Integration
Historical sources										I	E	E	R	
Scientific sources									I	E	R			
Literary sources											I	E		
Statistical sources												I		
Dictionaries	I						E			R				
• **Use print and electronic information access tools/resources**														
Building library catalog			I			E				R				
District library catalog					I			E		R				
Other library catalogs (e.g., public, college)								I		E	R			
Magazine Articles Summaries (MAS)								I		E	R			
NewsBank										I	E	R		
SIRS										I	E	R		
[Fill in local resources]														

I=Introduce   E=Expand   R=Refine/Reinforce

	K	1	2	3	4	5	6	7	8	9	10	11	12	Curricular Integration
Internet (WWW, AOL, Scholastic)				I				E		R				
Community Resources (individual/agency)				I					E		R			
• **Find information within sources using search features**														
Index (page, chapter, frames, tracks)				I		E		R						
Table of contents				I			R							

I=Introduce   E=Expand   R=Refine/Reinforce

	K	1	2	3	4	5	6	7	8	9	10	11	12	Curricular Integration
Chapter or section headings				I										
Navigational features (guidewords, search screens, find commands, cross references, bookmarks)				I						E				
• Scan, screen, and select appropriate resources														
Distinguish fiction from nonfiction		I				E				R				
Apply filtering criteria such as availability; currency; level of sophistication (suitability); primary/secondary source; point of view or bias; scope or depth; reliability/ accuracy; appropriateness (ethical)						I		E		R				
Prepare working bibliography or research log									I	E	R			

I=Introduce   E=Expand   R=Refine/Reinforce

Stage Three

Process the Information

	K	1	2	3	4	5	6	7	8	9	10	11	12	Curricular Integration
• Interpret the information within a source														
Read, view, listen to the information				I	E									
Use features within information source (outline, subtopic, hyperlink, photograph, video, caption, graph, chart)				I		E								
• Evaluate the relevance and usefulness of the information														
Use critical reading, viewing, listening techniques (Seven Quick Ways to Evaluate Information)							I		E		R			
• Extract relevant information														
Record information using techniques such as														
notetaking			I			E				R				
photocopying/highlighting														
copying/pasting														
interviewing														
video/audio recording														

I=Introduce   E=Expand   R=Refine/Reinforce

	K	1	2	3	4	5	6	7	8	9	10	11	12	Curricular Integration
scanning														
downloading														
drawing														
collecting artifacts														
Record bibliographic information for sources used		I				E				R				
Use information ethically														
Observe copyright laws (plagiarism)					I			E		R				
Quote/cite properly					I					E	R			
Observe Acceptable Use Agreement guidelines					I			E		R				
Analyze the information (Fill to meet local needs)		I				E				R				

I=Introduce   E=Expand   R=Refine/Reinforce

Stage Four

Create and Communicate Results

	K	1	2	3	4	5	6	7	8	9	10	11	12	Curricular Integration
• Organize/synthesize information from multiple sources using														
Logical sequence				I				E		R				
Storyboard		I			E					R				
Outline														
Web														
Other graphic organizers (flow chart, table)														
• Create a product to communicate the information using														
Computer basics	I				E			E						
Keyboarding					I	E		I						
Word processing					I			E		R			R	
Database								I		E				
Spreadsheet								I		E				
Graph/chart			I			E				R				
Visuals (poster, transparency)														

I=Introduce   E=Expand   R=Refine/Reinforce

	K	1	2	3	4	5	6	7	8	9	10	11	12	Curricular Integration
Presentation software										I				
Draw/paint software	I													
Multimedia	I				E									
Audio														
Video					I									
[Add additional product elements]														
•														
•														
•														
•														
•														
• Cite all sources used														
Prepare a bibliography (works cited)					I			E		R				

I=Introduce E=Expand R=Refine/Reinforce

Stage Five

Assess Process and Product

	K	1	2	3	4	5	6	7	8	9	10	11	12	Curricular Integration
• Evaluate the process			I			E				R				
• Evaluate the product			I			E				R				

I=Introduce   E=Expand   R=Refine/Reinforce

PART II:
MODEL LESSONS AND UNITS FOR ELEMENTARY CLASSES

OVERVIEW

The model lessons in Part II can be integrated with a classroom curriculum. They are based on the philosophy that information literacy objectives need to be taught within the context of classroom content. While the lessons that infuse information skills into science and social studies lessons are specific to the Iowa City Community School District curriculum, the objectives and lessons can be modified to fit the curriculum of any elementary school. The lessons in these chapters are of two types. Those in Section A can be adapted to any curricular area; those in Section B are tied to curricular content. All of these lessons can easily be adapted to fit local curricular needs.

Section A begins with four lessons on searching the electronic library catalog. As with other skills and concepts in the information literacy curriculum, the use of the automated library catalog is taught as part of a content-based unit designed collaboratively by the classroom teacher and the library media specialist. Because the library catalog will be the first electronic search tool for many students, the lessons are spelled out in some detail with ample opportunity for practice. These lessons provide an introduction to most of the strategies common to all electronic tools, including key-word searching; use of Boolean logic; search, sort, select; and truncation. The various components of these lessons should be taught at developmentally appropriate ages as determined by the library media specialist and teacher. The curriculum matrix displays suggested levels. The lesson on indexes introduces students to the structure and use of indexes to books and encyclopedias, both print and online. Ideally the examples used will tie into classroom projects so that the students have an incentive to learn to use an index effectively.

Finally, the introduction to computer graphics gives students the opportunity to create an electronic product, thereby practicing effective communication of information and gaining confidence in the use of computer graphic programs.

The lessons in Section B and Section C have explicit subject content, but the format and the projects can be adapted to any subject. If there is a good fit between the content of a lesson and the school curriculum, the lessons are ready to use. Otherwise, the teacher and library media specialist will find that an adaptation of the materials is more interesting to the students as well as more effective in developing information literacy skills.

All elements of the information literacy model are touched on each time a research lesson is done. For example, in all lessons students need to have a clear idea of the information problem to be solved. However, in many cases the teacher will make a very specific assignment for a particular element. Sometimes selected sources of information will already be identified for students, especially if the goal is to learn to use a particular resource such as an electronic encyclopedia. Consequently, the information literacy objectives of the lessons may focus on two or three elements of the model and not include a goal for the others. This does not mean that these other objectives should be ignored, but rather that the emphasis in the particular lesson is elsewhere.

SECTION A:

LESSONS YOU CAN ADAPT TO ANY CURRICULAR AREA

5 DEVELOPING A PRESEARCH PLAN

AUDIENCE

Third grade. This lesson should be taught whenever the students are ready to begin using an electronic tool.

INSTRUCTIONAL OBJECTIVE

The learner will use presearch planning strategies and procedures to fill out a presearch planning guide before doing a search on the library catalog. Note: some keyboarding skill is a prerequisite to this lesson.

INFORMATION LITERACY OBJECTIVE

Define the Information Need

Identify clearly the problem to be solved.

Locate Information

Generate key words to assist in searching.

MATERIALS NEEDED

- Presearch Planning Guide sheets for each student or group of students
- Library Catalog Presearch Planning Guide sheet
- General to Specific model
- Completed Presearch Planning Guides (pages 82-85) and others created by media specialist from template to match individual needs.
- Sample topics, using the Presearch Planning Guide form

ANTICIPATORY SET

You will soon be using the library catalog to look up information on _____[topic assigned by teacher]. To successfully locate this information you will need to do some planning before you go to the computer. Today you will learn how to plan a library catalog search.

INSTRUCTIONAL INPUT/MODELING

Each student answers the following questions:

1. What is the information problem? What question am I trying to answer? What is my topic? Model writing this into the Presearch Planning Guide on the overhead projector.
2. What key word or key phrase describes my topic?
   - The terms key word and key phrase refer to the most important word or words in a question and can be the name of a person, place or thing. Give examples of key words and phrases, and explain to the students that this will probably be the term(s) they will use the most often when gathering data.
   - Remind students to make sure that they know how to spell their key words correctly before going to the computer!
3. Have them ask, What are some general and specific related words that I can use in my search? (Show General to Specific model.)
   - General words broaden a search. Example: mammals instead of cats.
     (Show completed presearch guides.)
   - Specific words narrow a search and are often the quickest way to find the information needed. (Show transparencies.)
4. What type of information do I hope to find—text, number facts, pictures, maps, charts? Model writing this on the Presearch Planning Guide on the overhead projector.

CHECK FOR UNDERSTANDING

Exercise I: Instruct the students to practice making questions out of information problems (working in pairs). If possible, they should use problems related to the topic being studied. (These will need to be determined in advance by the classroom teacher and media specialist.)

Example #1: You need to find out if there is a dog breed called the flat-coated retriever.
   The question could be, What is a flat-coated retriever?

Example #2: The teacher says you need to find information on weapons used in the Middle Ages.
   The question could be, What weapons were used in the Middle Ages?

Example #3: You should find out how to tell a dolphin from a porpoise.
   The question could be, How are dolphins different from porpoises?

Example #4: You need to locate the state of Rhode Island and find out which parts of the state get the most rain.

The question could be, Where is Rhode Island and which part of the state gets the most rain?

Exercise II: General or Specific?

Students work in pairs to put the following word pairs into the correct category (general or specific):

1. dogs; golden retrievers
2. weather; tornadoes
3. Native Americans; Shawnee
4. blue whales; mammals
5. basketball; Chicago Bulls
6. Michigan; United States
7. cougars; wild cats
8. hamsters; pets

Exercise III: Ask the students which formats would provide the most useful information for the topics below? They can work in pairs. Choices are text, number facts, charts, pictures, and maps. (Use the Presearch Planning Guide on the overhead.)

Example: Flat-coated retriever (pictures, text)

Example: Weapons in the Middle Ages (pictures, text)

Example: Dolphins and porpoises—differences (pictures, text)

Example: Rhode Island—location and rainfall amounts (maps, charts, number facts)

GUIDED PRACTICE

Pass out the Presearch Planning Guide sheets. Have the students fill them out. Assist as needed. Emphasize that these sheets should be kept in the research folder and used later at the computer and in evaluating the final project.

To use the transparencies for the presearch planning lessons on CD-ROM:

1. Open the CD-ROM and go to the Chapter 5 Folder.
2. Click to open the Folder.
3. Scroll to the item you want.
4. Click to open.

Presearch Planning Guide for the Library Catalog

Name: _____

My topic is: _____

I want to answer this question: _____

_____

_____?

Key Word/ Phrase

General Related Words	Specific Related Words

I am looking for this information format (check all that apply):

Print: ❏ Text   ❏ Number facts   ❏ Charts

Nonprint ❏ Pictures   ❏ Maps

Presearch Planning Lesson for the Library Catalog

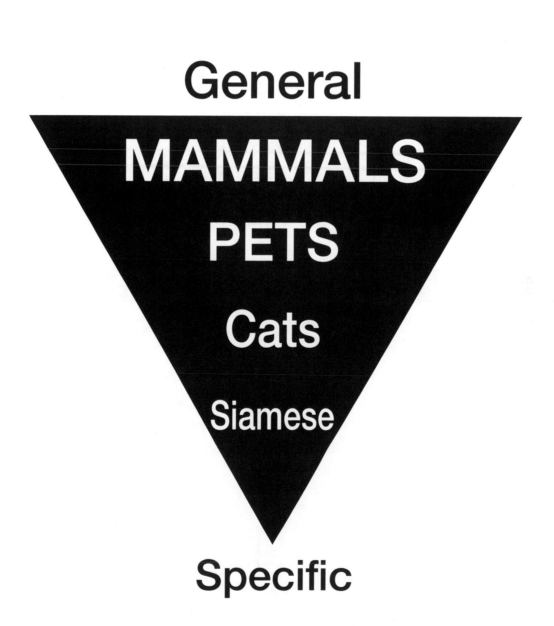

General

MAMMALS

PETS

Cats

Siamese

Specific

Presearch Planning Guide for the Library Catalog

Name: _____

My topic is: <u>the state of Michigan</u>

I want to answer this question: <u>What are the main crops grown in</u>
<u>the state of Michigan?</u>

General Related Words	Specific Related Words
United States	Corn
Agriculture	Apples
Farming	Cherries
Crops	Blueberries
Food	

I am looking for this information format (check all that apply):

Print: ☑ Text   ☑ Number facts   ☐ Charts

Nonprint   ☐ Pictures   ☐ Maps

Presearch Planning Guide for the Library Catalog

Name: _____

My topic is: <u>the birthstone for the month of May—the Emerald</u>

I want to answer this question: <u>What are the characteristics of the</u>
<u>Emerald?</u>

Key Word/
Phrase
Emerald

General Related Words	Specific Related Words
Minerals	Ruby
Birthstones	Diamond
Jewels	
Jewelry	
Gems	

I am looking for this information format (check all that apply):

Print: ☑ Text ☐ Number facts ☐ Charts

Nonprint ☑ Pictures ☐ Maps

Presearch Planning Guide for the Library Catalog

Name: _____

My topic is: <u>weapons in the Middle Ages</u>

I want to answer this question: <u>What were the names and</u>
<u>characteristics of some weapons used in the Middle Ages?</u>

> ### Key Word/ Phrase
> *Middle Ages*

General Related Words	Specific Related Words
Medieval *Arms* *Armor* *Weapons*	*Bow* *Arrow* *Sword*

I am looking for this information format (check all that apply):

Print: ☑ Text ☐ Number facts ☐ Charts

Nonprint ☑ Pictures ☐ Maps

Presearch Planning Guide for the Library Catalog

Name: _____

My topic is: <u>tornadoes</u>_____

I want to answer this question: <u>How do tornadoes form and what parts</u>
<u>of the United States have the most tornadoes?</u>_____

_____

Key Word/
Phrase
Tornado

General Related Words	Specific Related Words
Weather	*Cyclones*
Storms	*Twisters*
Disasters	*Waterspouts*
Wind	*Funnel clouds*
Thunderstorms	

I am looking for this information format (check all that apply):

Print: ☑ Text ☐ Number facts ☑ Charts

Nonprint ☐ Pictures ☑ Maps

6 SEARCHING THE CATALOG

The lessons that follow were designed to be used with the Macintosh version of the Winnebago Catalog program. The concepts and skills will be the same regardless of the automated system in place. Certain procedures will need to be modified to fit the local program.

OVERVIEW LESSON

INSTRUCTIONAL OBJECTIVE

The media specialist will use the author, title, and key-word lessons in large or small groups for instruction in using the library catalog. Modeling examples may be selected from the media center collection to fit the skill addressed in the lessons and to integrate with the curricular unit.

INFORMATION LITERACY OBJECTIVE

Locate Information

Students will practice skills that will enable them to find information using the electronic catalog.

MATERIALS NEEDED

- Access to library-catalog computer workstation
- Large screen projection capabilities
- Overhead projector
- Transparency: Library Catalog Lesson
- Transparency: Library Catalog Computer Lesson

PREREQUISITE SKILL CONSIDERATIONS FOR THE FOLLOWING LESSONS.

Information and Location Skills

- Recognition/interpretation of call number
- Location in library arrangement by call number
- Recognition of material type
- Definition of author and title
- Definition of key words/key phrases

Computer Skills and Terminology

- Scrolling
- Point, click, drag

- Window manipulation
- Active window/pull down/pop-up menus
- Title bar (striped)
- Moving and resizing to move back and forth in windows
- Close box
- Highlight selection—click to select or command/click on keyboard
- Still-searching clock
- Stop-search key command
- Pull-down menu and keyboard access
- Exit procedure

SEARCH/SORT/SELECT—AUTHORS

AUDIENCE
Elementary school children at point of need.

INSTRUCTIONAL OBJECTIVE
Student will search for an author using the author's last name.
Student will select desired title of author's work.
Process will include the search, sorting a field, and selection of material.

PREREQUISITE SKILL
Locate materials by call number
Dewey category recognition

INFORMATION LITERACY OBJECTIVE

Locate Information

INSTRUCTIONAL INPUT/MODELING

Search
On Card Catalog window

1. To the right of source click one time in circle preceding Author.
2. Type [last name] (space) [first name] of author, as much as known.
   - Name need not be in capitals.
   - Correct spelling helps in the search.
3. Click on Find

Notes

- Wild Card/truncation is not applicable or as useful for authors.
- Illustrators may be searched just as authors.
- Use of capital letters is unnecessary.
- Correct spelling is essential.
- Material types are helpful for location.

Sort

On the Materials Found window:

- Use the scroll bar to see additional listings.
- Sort by clicking on the title-field column if many titles are listed.
- Sort by clicking on call number field for nonfiction, easy, fiction, print, and nonprint.
- "Copies in" is indicated on far right column. The number in front of the slash indicates the number of items available; the number after the slash indicates the number of copies owned.

Select

- Highlight material needed by clicking once.
- Double click on item for more information and notes about material.
- Scroll down itemized list for additional subject headings or key words.
- If fewer than five items are needed, write down the call number and title on paper (see form on page 95) and locate items on shelf.
- Print the bibliography for five or more items.

Refine Search

- Check spelling of author's name.
- If author's name is not on window, go back to Card Catalog window and click on browse window to find author's name, use scroll bar.

SEARCH/SORT/SELECT—TITLES

INSTRUCTIONAL OBJECTIVE

Students will locate material by using the title of the material.

INSTRUCTIONAL INPUT/MODELING

Search

On the Card Catalog window:
1. To the right of Source, click once on the title button.
2. Type the title of the material wanted.
3. Click on the Find button.

Notes:

- Correct spelling is essential; capitalization is not important.
- "A," "An," and "The" as first words are automatically ignored. The search will list these titles by the second word.
- Numbers may be spelled out as words or entered as numerals.
- Abbreviated words do not need to be spelled out. The program automatically adjusts for all filing rules.

Sort

Since the patron is looking for an exact match, the sort process is not useful.

Select

On the Materials Found window:
If the item is a part of the collection, the title will be highlighted.

- Double click on the item for more information and notes about the material.
- If no further information is needed:

1. Note the call number of the item.
2. Check to see if the material is available by noting the "Copies In" column to the far right. The number in front of the slash indicates the number of items available; the number after the slash indicates the number of copies owned.

If the item is not a part of the collection or if the title has been misspelled, an alert box will appear stating, "No materials were found. Try using the browse window to find what you are looking for."

- Check to make sure the spelling is correct.
- The Browse feature may be helpful when the exact title is not known.
- It may be helpful in listing other titles that have similar titles or topics. Should the exact title not be in the collection, the most efficient plan would be to begin a key-word search.

SEARCH/SORT/SELECT—KEY WORDS

INSTRUCTIONAL OBJECTIVE
Students will search for materials using key words or key phrases.

INFORMATION LITERACY OBJECTIVE

Locate Information

INSTRUCTIONAL INPUT/MODELING

Search
On the Card Catalog window:
1. To the right of Source, key word will automatically be selected.
2. Type the key word or key phrase. Correct spelling is essential; capitalization is not important.
3. Click on the Find button.

Search Options

- Searches can be conducted using 1) plural, 2) singular, and 3) truncation "Wild Card" * options. The Wild Card (Shift *) will check all searchable fields, producing the greatest number of material choices. These fields can be searched after at least three letters of the key word or phrase are entered. Show examples of each kind of search. The user should see an increased number of choices if searches are completed in the following order.

    Examples: Pioneers, pioneer, pioneer*, pio*

    Kangaroos, kangaroo, kangaroo*, kan*

Choose examples that relate to content being taught.

- The greatest success will probably occur using a singular word with the wild card option. While the largest list appears with just the three letters and the wild card, many items are not at all related to the original topic.
- The search may take some time. The words "Still Searching" will show at the bottom of the screen during the search.

The Materials Found window appears with a list of materials that include the key word or phrase.

- The number of items found is listed at the bottom of the window.

- "Search Complete" will appear when the search is finished.
- Using the scroll bar allows all choices to be viewed.

Sort
- Click on the column name marked "Call Number." A sort by call number will organize material so that the patron can distinguish between nonfiction and fiction material.
- Further sorting on the Material Type may assist the patron.

Select
- Double click on the item for more information and notes about the material.
- Check material availability by noting the column to the far right "Copies In."

Related Searches

When the search does not produce the number of items desired, it is recommended that the patron consult the presearch planning guide for related words or phrases.

1. Click on New Search at the Card Catalog window.
2. Type a new key word or phrase.
3. Click on the Find button

   Examples: "cat" after trying "kitten"
   "mountain lion" after trying "puma"

If the search is still unsuccessful, conduct a logic search. Refer to the Logic Search option. The flow chart that follows may be used to review the search process with students, including the three different types of searches.

To use the transparencies for the Library Catalog Lesson and a copy of the search on CD-ROM:

1. Open the CD-ROM and go to the Chapter 6 Folder.
2. Click to open the Folder.
3. Scroll to the item you want
4. Click to open.

Library Catalog Lesson

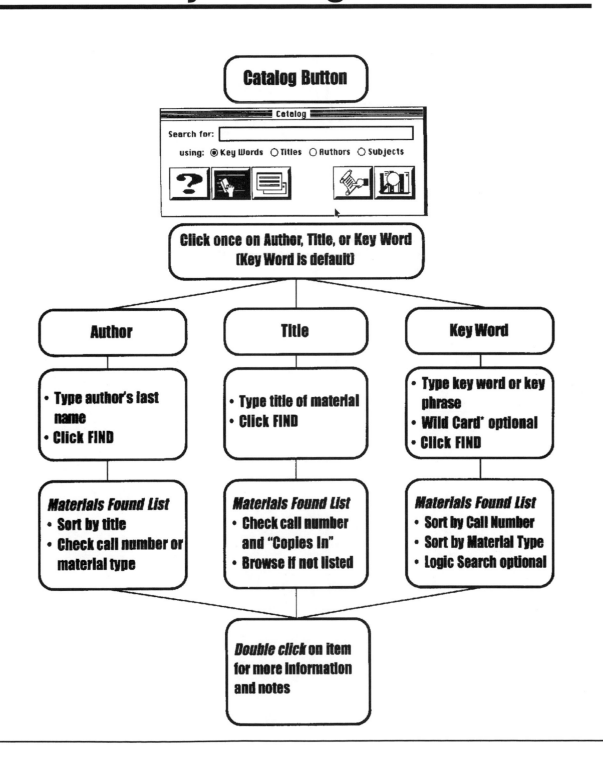

Catalog Button

Click once on Author, Title, or Key Word (Key Word is default)

Author

Title

Key Word

- Type author's last name
- Click FIND

- Type title of material
- Click FIND

- Type key word or key phrase
- Wild Card* optional
- Click FIND

Materials Found List
- Sort by title
- Check call number or material type

Materials Found List
- Check call number and "Copies In"
- Browse if not listed

Materials Found List
- Sort by Call Number
- Sort by Material Type
- Logic Search optional

Double click on item for more information and notes

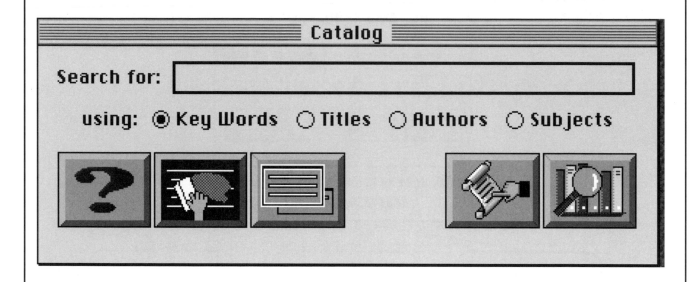

Sample Call Slip for Library Catalog Materials:

After evaluating the list of resources on the Materials Found window, it is recommended that users record the call numbers and titles so they can go to the shelf and find these materials. **If the list is five or fewer record this information on the call slips provided.** Be sure to include the complete call number. If the list is longer than five items it may be printed following the directions in specific catalog numbers.

Call Number _____   _____

Title _____

Call Number _____   _____

Title _____

Call Number _____   _____

Title _____

Call Number _____   _____

Title _____

Call Number _____   _____

Title _____

7 USING LOGIC TO SEARCH THE LIBRARY CATALOG

AUDIENCE

Students in the upper grades. Logic searches can be easily incorporated into the curriculum in the areas of language arts, science, and social studies. Cooperative planning is very important in this area of location and access skills.

INSTRUCTIONAL OBJECTIVE

The learner will use the Logic Search option of the library catalog to broaden or narrow a search for resources.

INFORMATION LITERACY OBJECTIVE

Locate Information

MATERIALS NEEDED

- Overhead projector
- Transparencies and activity sheets
- Access to library catalog
- Colored paper circles in blue and yellow; these may be laminated and used again. *Note*: Jelly Beans or other colored candies may be used instead of the colored paper circles.

ANTICIPATORY SET

The teacher or media specialist needs to review the following concepts prior to learning about the Logic Search option: library catalog; search strategy; presearch planning; defining key word; searching by key word, author, and title; browse option, and find option.

INPUT/MODELING

This series of lessons is divided into two sections. The first defines Boolean operators and gives students practice with Boolean terms and Venn diagrams using everyday objects and experiences. The lesson gives many choices; the media specialist should determine the prior knowledge of the learner group in order to customize. The second section applies this knowledge to logic searches using the library catalog.

Exercise I. Demonstrate the three search terms (Boolean operators AND, OR, and AND NOT) by conducting the following class activities.

1. Define Boolean operators using paper circles for actual hands-on experience (Use Logic Searches on pages 101–105.). This may serve as a demonstration or provide actual hands-on experience.

2. Use two groups of students as the search "terms"; for example group A—students in the 6th grade, group B—students wearing glasses. Begin the demonstration by defining these groups. Ask students who are members of group A to stand, have them sit down, ask the members of group B to stand, and then have them sit down. Ask those to stand who are in

   group A OR group B
   group A AND group B
   group A AND NOT B
   group B AND NOT A

   Introduce the concept of the Venn diagram (pages 106–107.). Venn Diagrams are used as visual representations of searching and grouping concepts. On the overhead, record the results of the demonstration by drawing Venn diagrams. Emphasize the concept of each term.

   OR: broadens or expands a search
   AND: narrows a search
   AND NOT: limits a search

3. Conduct similar demonstrations using other groups as search terms, for example, students who play a musical instrument, have brown eyes, walk to school, have a pet, like pizza, and so forth. Record the results using Venn diagrams. Three search terms or groups may be used at once.

Exercise II. Instruction and practice using the Logic Search window.

1. Using transparency Logic Search Computer Window (page 108) or going directly to a catalog monitor, explain the layout of the "More Choices" screen.

   • "More Choices" is opened by clicking that option on the opening catalog window.
   • One, two, or three lines may be used for a search.
   • For each line used, two elements must be defined:
     Source (key word, title, author, subject, call number)
     Logic (one of the Boolean operators—AND, OR, AND NOT)

- More choices for Source and for Logic are found by clicking the pop-up menu.
- Browse, Find, and Help options are all available.

For call numbers, media specialists will need to instruct the students in the designations used by individual libraries as call number prefixes for nonprint materials.

2. Model and explain the Logic Search strategy using the terms Cats and Dogs and the accompanying Venn diagrams (pages 109–116). This search shows the results of a search in an Iowa school catalog. The media specialist may prefer to customize the topic for a particular collection or use other search terms.

3. Model and explain the following search strategies (page 117). Look up the terms and record the number of items found for each. Define items found as those that successfully meet the criteria.

It is strongly suggested that the media specialist conduct these searches prior to instruction to be fully aware of the results unique to the school's collection. Customizing the list according to the classroom curriculum is preferable.

CHECK FOR UNDERSTANDING

1. Students work in pairs. Have each student determine two or three terms for a search, share them with his or her partner, and have the partner draw Venn diagrams to show the results of each Boolean operation.

2. Students working in teams could create key-word search exercises to try to stump other teams. The students select terms, combine them with AND, OR, or AND NOT, and have the opposing team draw the correct Venn diagram to represent their search statement.

3. Students may create Venn diagrams about their favorite athletes, TV and movie stars, singers, etc. *For example*: musician AND singer; on TV NOT movies; National League OR American League, NOT championship winner.

GUIDED PRACTICE

1. Venn Diagram activity sheets (pages 118–119)
2. Searching activity sheet—to be completed using the library catalog (page 120)
3. Boolean Operators activity sheet—may be used as an evaluative tool (page 121)

To use the transparencies and activities for the Logic Search on CD-ROM:

1. Open the CD-ROM and go to the Chapter 7 Folder.
2. Click to open the Folder.
3. Select the item you want.
4. Click to open.

Logic Search Using Paper Circles

These paper circles represent items we might be searching for in the library catalog or other electronic tool.

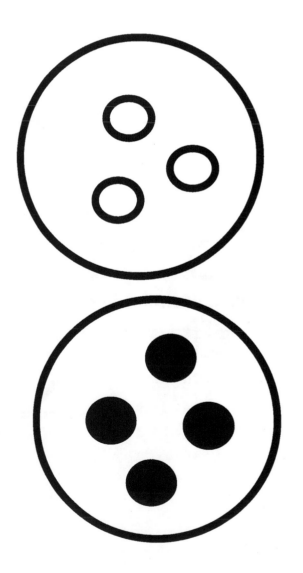

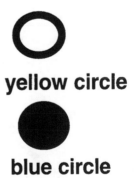

yellow circle

blue circle

Logic Search Yellow AND Blue

Searching for yellow AND blue will give us no circles. No circles are both blue and yellow.

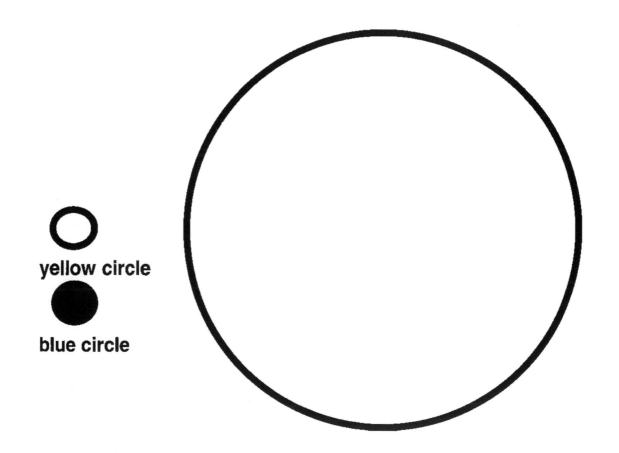

yellow circle

blue circle

Logic Search Yellow OR Blue

Searching for blue OR yellow will give us all of the circles. All circles are either blue or yellow.

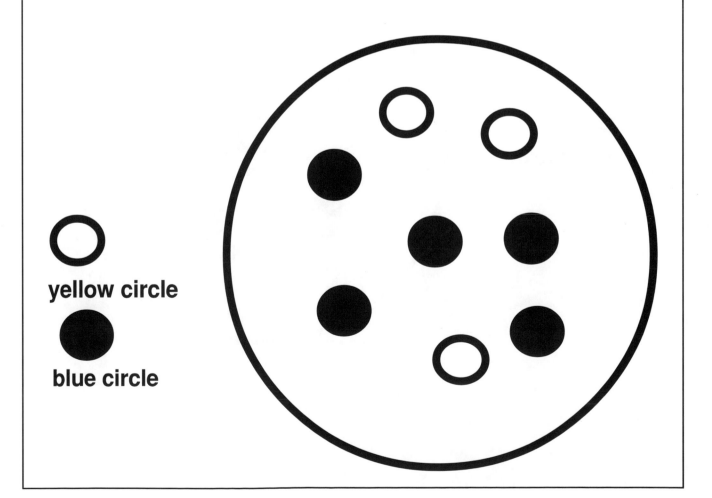

yellow circle

blue circle

Logic Search Blue AND NOT Yellow

Blue AND NOT Yellow will show only the blue circles. No yellow circles will be selected.

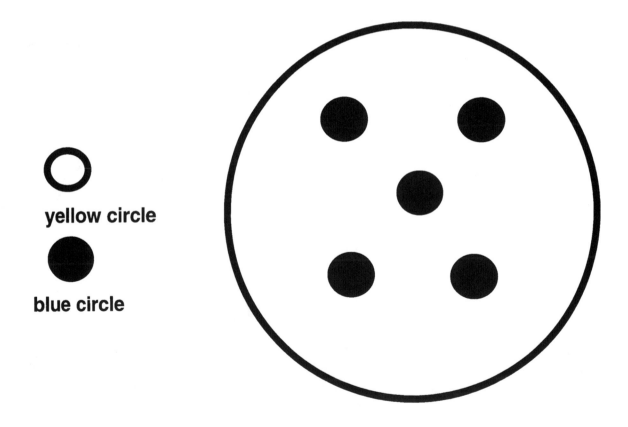

yellow circle

blue circle

Logic Search Yellow AND NOT Blue

Yellow AND NOT Blue will show only the yellow circles. No blue circles will be selected.

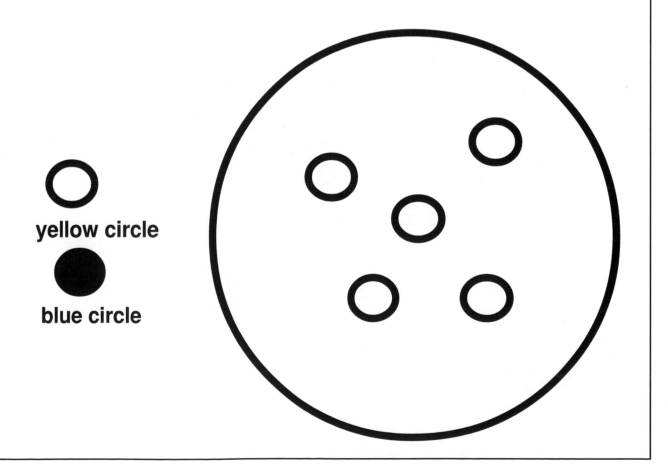

yellow circle

blue circle

Logic Search – Venn Diagrams

A OR B

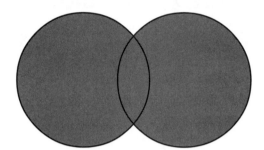

A AND B

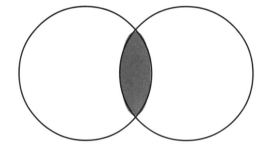

A AND NOT B

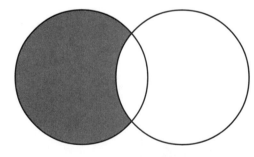

B AND NOT A

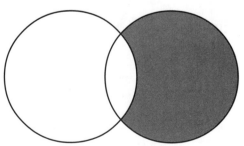

Logic Search—Venn Diagrams

____OR ____

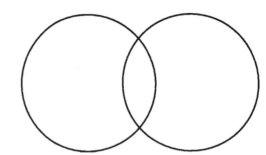

____ AND ____

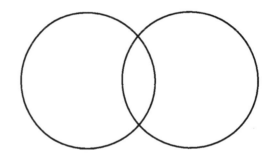

____ AND NOT ____

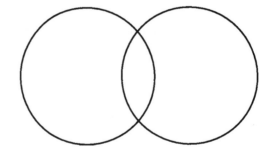

____ AND NOT ____

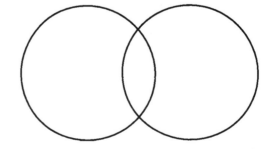

Logic Search Computer Window

More Choices

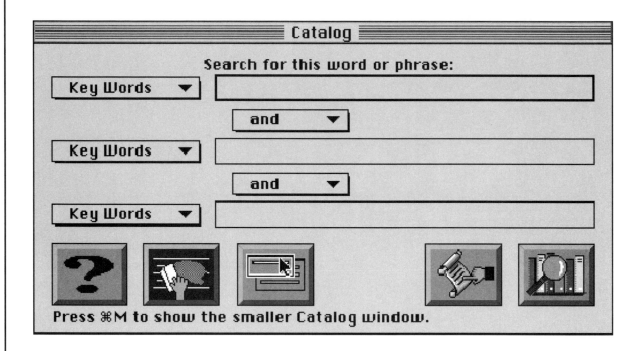

Logic Searches

Books about Dogs

A Dog's Body
What Kind of Dog Is That?
ASPCA Puppy Guide
Dogs Working for People
Domesticated Animals

Books about Cats

Album of Cats
Raising Your Cat
Cats: Little Tigers in Your
        House
A Cat's Body
ASPCA Kitten Guide
Domesticated Animals

How many books does this library have that contain information about dogs? How many about cats? Note that one book appears on both lists because it contains dog information and cat information.

Logic Searches (Dogs AND Cats)

A Dog's Body
What Kind of Dog Is That?
ASPCA Puppy Guide
Dogs Working for People
Domesticated Animals

Album of Cats
Raising Your Cat
Cats: Little Tigers in Your
  House
A Cat's Body
ASPCA Kitten Guide
Domesticated Animals

**What books will be found for Dogs AND Cats?
Only *one* book — *Domesticated Animals.***

Logic Searches (Dogs OR Cats)

A Dog's Body
What Kind of Dog Is That?
ASPCA Puppy Guide
Dogs Working for People
Domesticated Animals

Album of Cats
Raising Your Cat
Cats: Little Tigers in Your House
A Cat's Body
ASPCA Kitten Guide
Domesticated Animals

What books will be found for Dogs OR Cats? All of them!

A Dog's Body
What Kind of Dog Is That?
ASPCA Puppy Guide
Dogs Working for People
Domesticated Animals

Album of Cats
Raising Your Cat
Cats: Little Tigers in Your House
A Cat's Body
ASPCA Kitten Guide
Domesticated Animals

Logic Search: Venn Diagrams
(Dogs AND NOT Cats)

A Dog's Body
What Kind of Dog Is That?
ASPCA Puppy Guide
Dogs Working for People
Domesticated Animals

Album of Cats
Raising Your Cat
Cats: Little Tigers in Your
     House
A Cat's Body
ASPCA Kitten Guide
Domesticated Animals

What books will be found for Dogs AND NOT Cats?

A Dog's Body
What Kind of Dog Is That?
ASPCA Puppy Guide
Dogs Working for People

What books will be found for Cats AND NOT Dogs?
Will this search be the same or different?

Logic Search: Venn Diagrams (Dogs AND Cats)

Dogs AND Cats

The shaded area shows books that have information about both dogs and cats in them. This is fewer books than adding up the number of books about dogs and the number of books about cats. AND narrows a search. It gives fewer "hits."

Logic Search: Venn Diagrams (Dogs OR Cats)

The shaded area shows books that have information about either dogs or cats in them. This is the same number of books as adding up the number of books about dogs and the number of books about cats. OR broadens a search. It gives more "hits."

<u>Logic Search:</u> Venn Diagrams (Dogs AND NOT Cats)

Books about Dogs

Books about Cats

Dogs AND NOT Cats

Books about Dogs

Books about Cats

The shaded area shows books that have only dogs in them. If a book has information about dogs and cats in it, then it is ignored. AND NOT limits a search. It will produce fewer "hits."

Logic Search: Venn Diagrams (Cats AND NOT Dogs)

The shaded area shows books that have only cats in them. If a book has information about cats and dogs in it, then it is ignored. AND NOT limits a search. It will produce fewer "hits."

Logic Search—Key Words

Using the information you have learned about Boolean operators and logic searching, look up the following terms in the computer catalog:

Search Terms	Number of Items Found
1. Dogs	_____
Cats	_____
Dogs OR Cats	_____
Dogs AND Cats	_____
2. School	_____
Stories	_____
School AND Stories	_____
School AND Stories AND Everyone Books (or Easy Books)	_____
3. Presidents	_____
United States	_____
Presidents AND United States	_____
Presidents AND NOT United States	_____
4. Bears	_____
Bears AND NOT Fiction	_____
Bears AND Fiction	_____
Bears AND Everyone Books	_____

Name_____

Logic Search: Key Words

Use the Boolean operators AND, OR and AND NOT to create Venn diagrams representing the following search statements. Label the circles and shade them to fit

1. Dinosaurs AND NOT Tyrannosaurus

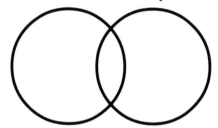

2. Music OR Jazz

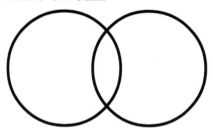

3. Pets AND NOT Dogs

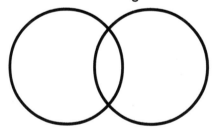

4. Farming AND Iowa

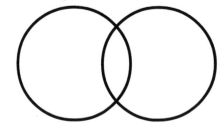

5. Boys AND Girls AND Teenagers

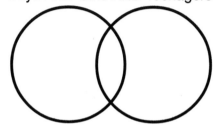

6. King of England OR Queen of England

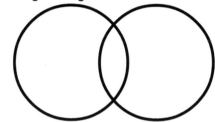

7. Sports AND NOT Football

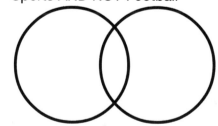

8. Inventor AND B (for Biography)

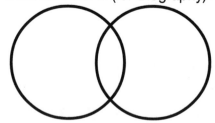

Name _____

Logic Search: Venn Diagrams

Draw Venn diagrams to represent the following search statements. Label the circles and shade them to fit the statement.

1. **Sports AND NOT Soccer**

2. **Rock music OR Rap music**

3. **Boys AND Girls**

4. **Bicycles OR Biking**

5. **Insects AND NOT Spiders**

Name_____

Logic Search: Key Words

Using the information you have learned about Boolean operators and logic searching, look up the following terms in the library catalog:

Search Terms	Number of Items Found

1. Tall tales   _____

    Paul Bunyan   _____

    Tall tales AND NOT Paul Bunyan   _____

2. Castles   _____

    Medieval   _____

    Castles AND Medieval   _____

    Castles OR Medieval   _____

3. Endangered   _____

    Plants   _____

    Animals   _____

    Endangered AND Plants   _____

    Endangered AND Animals   _____

    Endangered OR Plants AND NOT   _____

    Easy books or everybody books   _____

4. Mexico   _____

    New Mexico   _____

    Mexico AND NOT New Mexico   _____

    New Mexico AND NOT Mexico   _____

Name _____

Logic Searching

Use the library catalog to find the results from different sets of search terms. Record the terms searched and the number of records found for each Boolean operation.

1. Search terms: _____

   Number of Records: AND_____ OR_____AND NOT_____

2. Search terms: _____

   Number of Records: AND_____ OR_____AND NOT_____

3. Label and fill in the Venn diagram to show the results of each Boolean operation.

A AND NOT B

A AND B

A OR B

8 EVALUATING YOUR CATALOG SEARCH

AUDIENCE

Upper elementary students who have a working knowledge of how to use the library catalog. This activity could be integrated with a variety of projects in language arts, social studies, and other areas.

INFORMATION LITERACY OBJECTIVE

Locate Information

Determine best sources

INSTRUCTIONAL OBJECTIVE

The learner will determine whether a resource in the catalog is appropriate and relevant for a particular information need.

MATERIALS NEEDED

- Access to library catalog
- Large screen display device
- Transparencies
- Overhead projector
- Activity Sheets (Copies for small groups as determined by media specialist)

ANTICIPATORY SET

To be determined by the teacher or media specialist depending upon the curricular unit.

INPUT/MODELING

Stress to the students that the purpose of the library catalog is to help them identify resources—print and nonprint—that will fit their information needs.

Sometimes a search will yield many records, other times only one or a very small number. After each search is completed, the user should always make a practice of first sorting the list of resources. Next, scroll to the area of resources needed (call number, type/format). It is useful to look critically at the Itemized List window for each record in this area, especially when there are many records on a topic. Click on the highlighted item to see the full record. Carefully try to determine which resources would be the best to locate on the shelf first and use to find information.

There are four basic ways to compare and select the best source for a particular information need. (Use Evaluating Sources, page 125.)

1. fiction versus nonfiction (Use Evaluating Sources, page 126, 134.)
2. age (currency) of resource (Use Evaluating Sources, page 127.)
3. illustrations/visuals (Use Evaluating Sources, pages 128–131.) It will be necessary to use the transparencies with the card image (pages 129–131) at this point since the Itemized List window does not give the physical description of the resource. Students should learn the definition of each of the items listed in the physical description since "number of pages" is significant in many cases.
4. print versus nonprint (Use Evaluating Sources, page 130, 133.)

(Review by once again using page 125.)

Sometimes it is difficult to evaluate a source solely by the Itemized List or Card View screens, so it is important to look carefully at any source that has even remote possibilities.

CHECK FOR UNDERSTANDING

Ask students to turn to a partner and together try to name the four things to remember when evaluating sources on the screen list. Discuss these as a group.

GUIDED PRACTICE

Assign students to small groups. Give each group one packet with four activity sheets that show an information need and two possibilities of sources that could answer that need. Ask the students to

1. read the question carefully, considering which of the four considerations is critical to the question.
2. select the better of the two resources to use.

INDEPENDENT PRACTICE

To be determined in collaboration with the classroom teacher. The screens reproduced in this section are from the Winnebago Catalog program. Media specialists may wish to substitute screen shots from their own automated library catalog.

To use the transparencies and activities for Evaluation of Sources–Library Catalog on CD-ROM:

1. Open the CD-ROM and go to the Chapter 8 Folder.
2. Click to open.
3. Scroll to the item you want.
4. Click to open.

Evaluating Sources–Library Catalog

Fiction versus Non-Fiction

Age (Currency) of the Resource

Illustrations/Visuals

Print versus Nonprint

Evaluating Sources–Library Catalog

If factual information is needed regarding the Aztecs, which source would be most helpful?

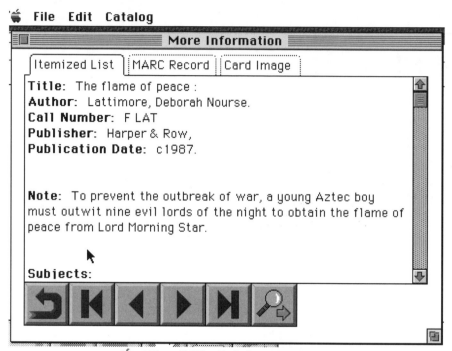

A

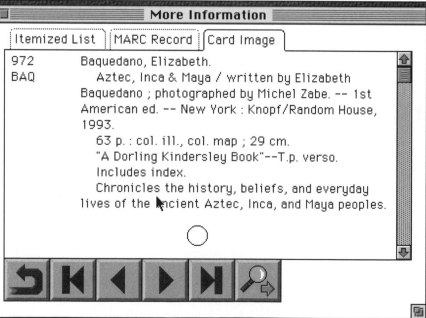

B

Evaluating Sources–Library Catalog

To learn about recent inventions, the first source to use would be...

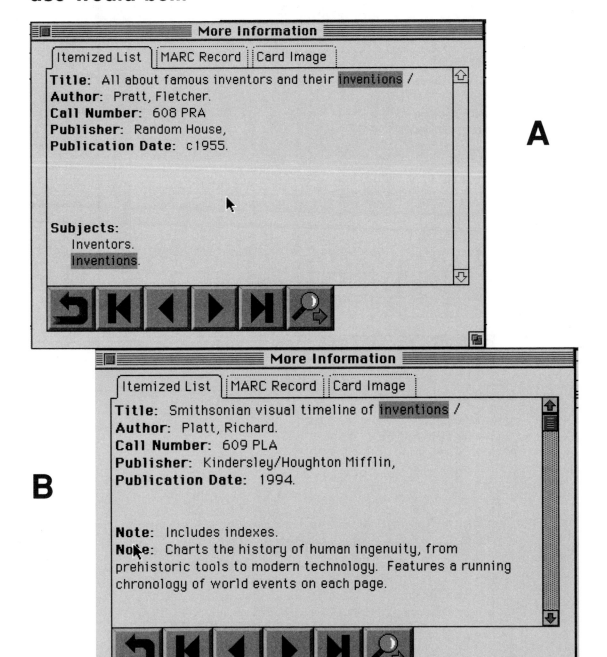

Evaluating Sources–Library Catalog

The group is doing a project and needs a map...

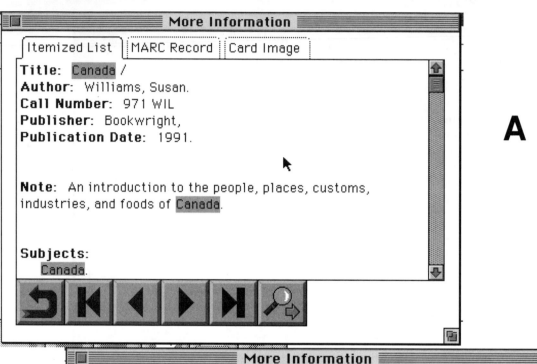

Evaluating Sources–Library Catalog

The group is doing a project and needs a map...

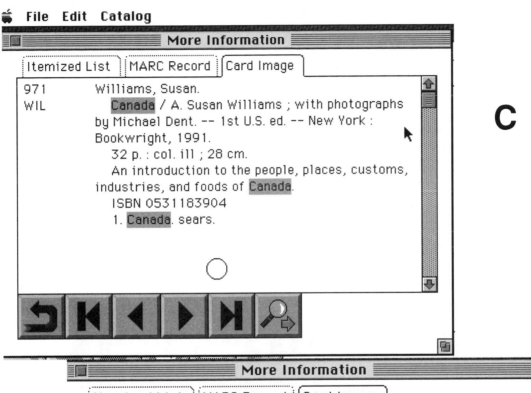

File   Edit   Catalog

More Information

Itemized List   MARC Record   Card Image

971   Williams, Susan.
WIL   Canada / A. Susan Williams ; with photographs
          by Michael Dent. -- 1st U.S. ed. -- New York :
          Bookwright, 1991.
              32 p. : col. ill ; 28 cm.
              An introduction to the people, places, customs,
          industries, and foods of Canada.
              ISBN 0531183904
              1. Canada. sears.

C

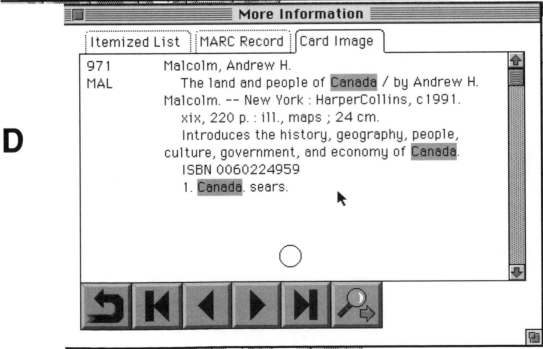

More Information

Itemized List   MARC Record   Card Image

971   Malcolm, Andrew H.
MAL   The land and people of Canada / by Andrew H.
          Malcolm. -- New York : HarperCollins, c1991.
              xix, 220 p. : ill., maps ; 24 cm.
              Introduces the history, geography, people,
          culture, government, and economy of Canada.
              ISBN 0060224959
              1. Canada. sears.

D

Evaluating Sources–Library Catalog

Your group wants to include some film of the countryside in a multimedia presentation about Iowa.

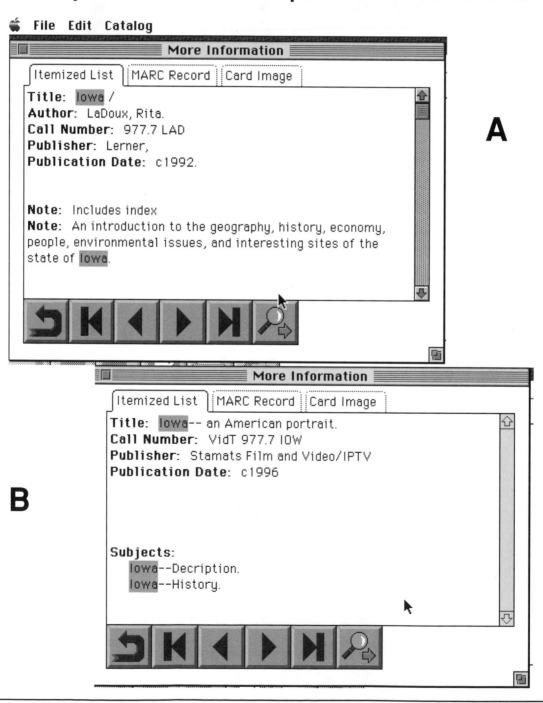

File Edit Catalog

More Information

| Itemized List | MARC Record | Card Image |

Title: Iowa /
Author: LaDoux, Rita.
Call Number: 977.7 LAD
Publisher: Lerner,
Publication Date: c1992.

Note: Includes index
Note: An introduction to the geography, history, economy, people, environmental issues, and interesting sites of the state of Iowa.

A

More Information

| Itemized List | MARC Record | Card Image |

Title: Iowa-- an American portrait.
Call Number: VidT 977.7 IOW
Publisher: Stamats Film and Video/IPTV
Publication Date: c1996

Subjects:
   Iowa--Decription.
   Iowa--History.

B

Evaluating Sources–Library Catalog

Your assignment asks for colored pictures of life in Mexico.

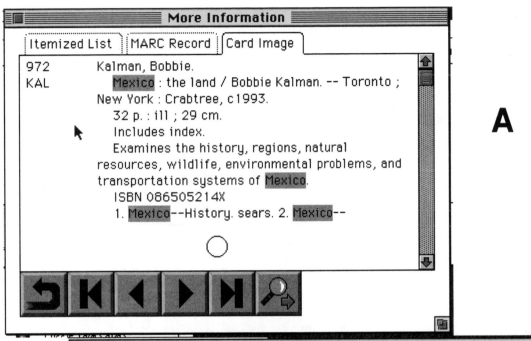

A

More Information

Itemized List | MARC Record | Card Image

972   Kalman, Bobbie.
KAL   Mexico : the land / Bobbie Kalman. -- Toronto ;
         New York : Crabtree, c1993.
             32 p. : ill ; 29 cm.
             Includes index.
             Examines the history, regions, natural
         resources, wildlife, environmental problems, and
         transportation systems of Mexico.
             ISBN 086505214X
             1. Mexico--History. sears. 2. Mexico--

B

More Information

Itemized List | MARC Record | Card Image

972   Rummel, Jack.
RUM   Mexico / Jack Rummel. -- New York : Chelsea
         House, c1990.
             127 p. : ill. (some col.) ; 21 cm.
             Surveys the history, topography, people, and
         culture of Mexico, with emphasis on its current
         economy, industry, and place in the political
         world.
             ISBN 0791011100
             1. Mexico. sears. 2. Mexico.

Press there to page down.

Evaluating Sources-Library Catalog

Your assignment asks for recent information on weather forecasting.

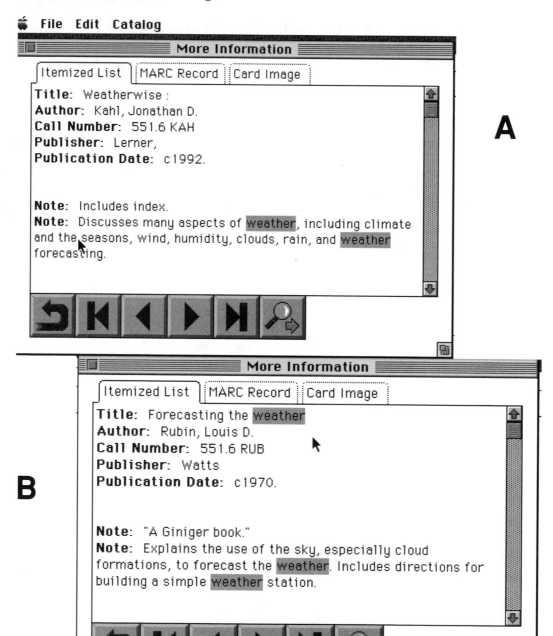

Evaluating Sources-Library Catalog

You want to get a sense of what it sounds like to be in the rain forest.

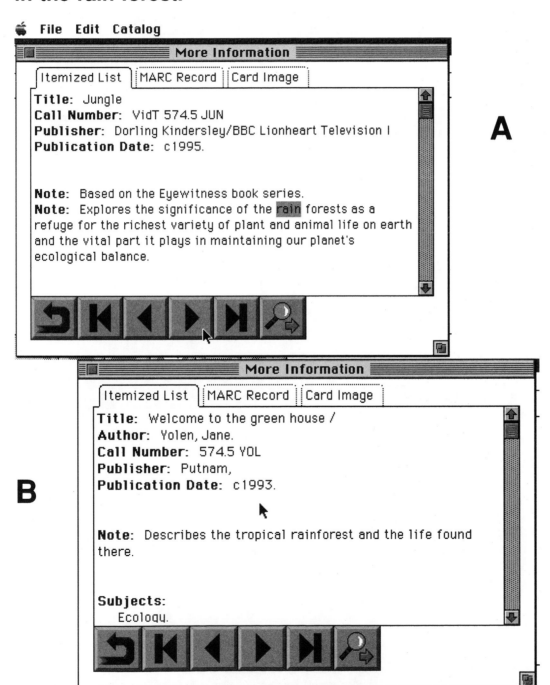

 File   Edit   Catalog

More Information

| Itemized List | MARC Record | Card Image |

Title: Jungle
Call Number: VidT 574.5 JUN
Publisher: Dorling Kindersley/BBC Lionheart Television I
Publication Date: c1995.

Note: Based on the Eyewitness book series.
Note: Explores the significance of the rain forests as a refuge for the richest variety of plant and animal life on earth and the vital part it plays in maintaining our planet's ecological balance.

A

More Information

| Itemized List | MARC Record | Card Image |

B

Title: Welcome to the green house /
Author: Yolen, Jane.
Call Number: 574.5 YOL
Publisher: Putnam,
Publication Date: c1993.

Note: Describes the tropical rainforest and the life found there.

Subjects:
Ecology.

Evaluating Sources-Library Catalog

Activty Sheet 4

If additional information is needed on the stegosaurus, which resource would be best?

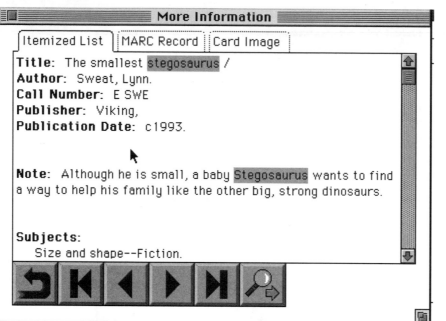

FORMATIVE EVALUATION OF LIBRARY CATALOG SEARCH

AUDIENCE
Students completing projects in language arts, social studies, science, or other subject areas.

INSTRUCTIONAL OBJECTIVE
The learner will evaluate the initial search using a checklist of criteria to further refine the search.

INFORMATION LITERACY OBJECTIVE

Assess Process and Product
Self-assess the search process for efficiency

MATERIALS NEEDED
- Information Literacy Model
- Copies and transparency of Student Evaluation of Search Process sheet

ANTICIPATORY SET
To be determined by the teacher or media specialist depending upon the curricular unit.

INPUT/MODELING
After doing a simple search or a logic search, it is very important to evaluate the search.

- Ask the question, "What do I need to do to refine my search based on what I have learned?"
- Never accept the first list of sources or the first search.
- Remember, every search can be improved. This is especially necessary if the search process isn't working as expected.

Here are some things for the students to ask themselves:

1. Does this list of sources appear to be what I expected or should I revisit my presearch planning guide?
2. Is a "logic search/more choices search" better? or is a "simple search" acceptable in this instance?
3. Did I get very few or no sources? If so,

- check spelling
- try singular form
- use wild card character (*) with at least the first three letters
- try different key words (more general)
- try Related Words
- change logic operators

  OR broadens

- try inferred key words
- browse subject headings of a few records to find new key words

4. Is the list too long? If so,
   - change logic operators
     —AND narrows
     —AND NOT limits
   - use more specific key words

CHECK FOR UNDERSTANDING

As a group, the students discuss some of the search experiences that they have had in the past. Which of the checklist items would have been helpful?

GUIDED PRACTICE

With students at patron stations, try searches on general topics, such as dinosaurs, bears, dogs, etc. Have students complete the Self-Evaluation of Completed Library Catalog Search (page 137).

To use files for Formative Evaluation of Library Catalog Search and Summative Evaluation of Library Catalog Search:

1. Open the CD-ROM and go to the Chapter 8 Folder.
2. Click to open the Folder.
3. Scroll down to the desired file.
4. Click to open

Student Name_____

Student Self-Evaluation of Completed Library Catalog Search

1. **How did the Presearch Planning Guide help me?**

2. **How well did my search strategy work?**

3. **If it didn't work, what was the problem?**

4. **Were adequate resources available? Could I find the information that I needed?**

5. **What would I change or do differently the next time I do a library catalog search**

SUMMATIVE EVALUATION OF LIBRARY CATALOG SEARCH

AUDIENCE

Students who have completed projects in language arts, social studies, science, or other subjects.

INSTRUCTIONAL OBJECTIVE

The learner will evaluate the completed search using a questionnaire.

INFORMATION LITERACY OBJECTIVE

Assess Process and Product

Reflect and adjust search strategies for future research.

MATERIALS NEEDED

- Copies of the Student Evaluation of Search Process form

ANTICIPATORY SET

To be determined by teacher or media specialist depending upon the curricular integration tie.

INPUT/MODELING

Emphasize to students that evaluation takes two forms. Tell them that one is the kind that you do as you are doing the search to get the materials—books, videos, film, etc.—that you need. The other is one that you do when you are finished with a project. This reflection gives you a chance to think back about what was good and what was unexpected.

Here are the kinds of question to think about:

1. How did the Presearch Planning Guide help?
2. How well did the search strategy work?
3. If it didn't work, what was the problem?
4. Were adequate resources available? Could I find the information that I needed?
5. What would I change or do differently the next time I do a search?

CHECK FOR UNDERSTANDING

Have the students tell a partner how they think this sheet is different from the other evaluations that they have done in the past. Share ideas.

GUIDED PRACTICE

Have students complete the Student Evaluation of Search Process (page 140).

Student Name _____

Student Evaluation of Search Process

1. Is the list of sources found what I expected or should I revisit my Presearch Planning Guide?

2. Is a "Logic Search/More Choices Search" better, or is a "Simple Search" acceptable in this instance?

3. Did I get very few or no sources?

   - check spelling
   - try singular form
   - use wild card character (*) with at least the first three letters
   - try different key words (more general)
   - try Related Words
   - change logic operators
        OR – broadens
   - try inferred key words
   - browse subject headings of a few records to find new keywords

4. Is the list too long?
   - change logic operators
        AND — narrows
        AND NOT — limits
   - use more specific key words

9 USING INDEXES

AUDIENCE
Grades 3 and up. Indexes are used in nearly all library research assignments. This lesson could be taught in conjunction with activities in many different content areas.

INSTRUCTIONAL OBJECTIVE
The learner will understand the arrangement, content, and purpose of an index.

MATERIALS NEEDED
- Overhead projector
- Nonfiction or reference books, preferably related to the curriculum, with indexes (make transparencies)
- Nonfiction books on a topic related to the curriculum
- Telephone book (make a transparency or use discarded phone books)
- Electronic encyclopedia (make a transparency of index)

INFORMATION LITERACY OBJECTIVE

Locate Information

ANTICIPATORY SET
To be determined by the teacher or media specialist based on the curricular unit.

INPUT/MODELING
An index is a list, usually alphabetical, that tells where information can be found. The advantage of using an index is that it helps to find information quickly and in a systematic manner.

Show several books that have indexes; discuss the time factor for finding specific information in a thick book without using an index. With each book find a topic and tell what page is listed in the index for that topic.

An index for a nonfiction book is usually arranged in alphabetical order. Show examples of indexes on transparencies made from books in your library media center.

Indexes for print sources usually conform to the rules for key-word searching. Review key-word (person-place-thing) rules. Show the telephone book. Discuss the alphabetical last-name arrangement of this familiar index. (Use a transparency made from local phone book.) Note the importance of correct spelling.

An index can also be a computerized database. Discuss alphabetical arrangement of the list of topics from an electronic encyclopedia in your library. Note that the library catalog is a computerized database with an index.

Some indexes contain subheadings as well as main headings. Use a transparency of an index with subheadings to point out a main heading followed by indented subheadings. Discuss the relationship of subheadings to the main heading and the time-saving factors involved in using subheadings to locate information quickly. Ask students to point out other main headings and subheadings.

The following aspects of indexes can be discussed if the media specialist determines it is necessary.

Some indexes contain cross-references. Use a transparency to illustrate cross-references leading the user to the correct terminology.

Individual indexes maintain consistency of format throughout. Notations for maps, illustrations, italics, and so forth are found in some indexes.

CHECK FOR UNDERSTANDING

Using a dictionary and a table of contents from a nonfiction book, determine if either is an example of an index. "Is it in alphabetical order? Does it give a location?"

GUIDED PRACTICE

Group students into twos or threes. Using a series of familiar nonfiction books (e.g., *Amazing Animals* or Grolier's Animals series), prepare a card for each book asking students to answer a question on a topic. Students will determine the key word in the question and locate the information in their books using the index. Students may also be asked to point out a topic with a subheading and a cross-reference, if found. The media specialist will check each group.

INDEPENDENT PRACTICE

To be determined in collaboration with the classroom teacher.

Index: Purpose and Arrangement

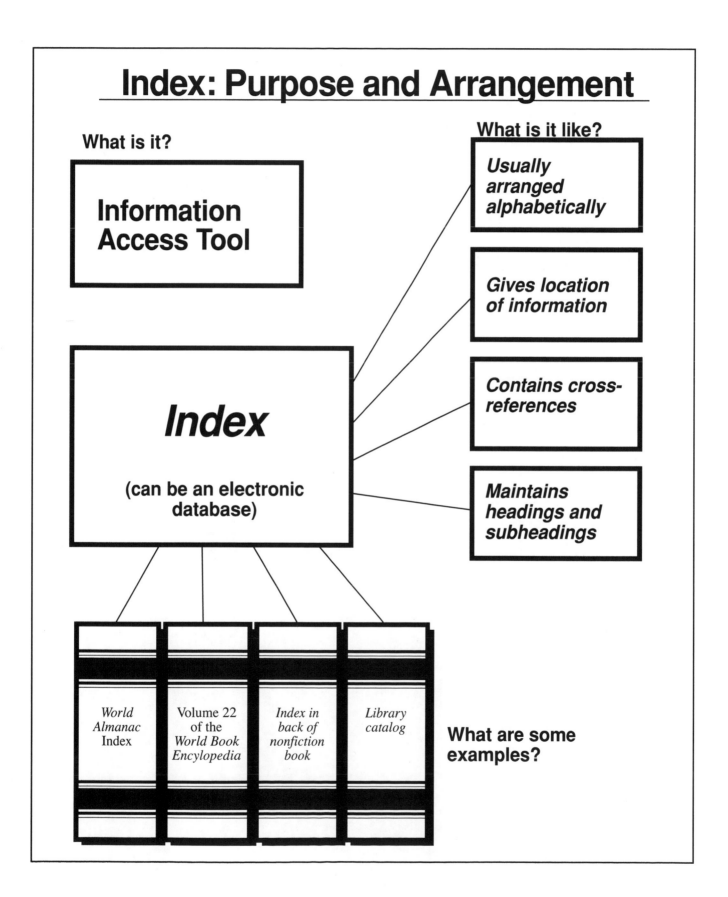

What is it?

Information Access Tool

Index

(can be an electronic database)

What is it like?

Usually arranged alphabetically

Gives location of information

Contains cross-references

Maintains headings and subheadings

World Almanac Index

Volume 22 of the World Book Encylopedia

Index in back of nonfiction book

Library catalog

What are some examples?

10 INTRODUCTION TO COMPUTER GRAPHICS

AUDIENCE

First grade. The students will learn various graphic and text tools to illustrate and complete a descriptive statement based on a book they have read in class. Individual student slides will be assembled into a slide show presentation.

INSTRUCTIONAL OBJECTIVES

Students will

1. manipulate a mouse as a computer input device.
2. make decisions about color and design using computer graphics.
3. incorporate text and voice into their design.
4. learn to run a Kid Pix or other electronic slide show.
5. gain confidence in using computer graphic and text tools.

INFORMATION LITERACY OBJECTIVE

Create and Communicate Results

Students will have an opportunity to create an electronic product.

Assess Process and Product

Students will be shown how to access their presentation on a computer for viewing by parents and classmates during back-to-school night.

INSTRUCTIONAL INPUT/MODELING

1. Students read *Freight Train* by Donald Crews (or another pattern book) with the classroom teacher. The classroom teacher will determine basic word recognition and reading strategies to incorporate. Students select a descriptive word to complete the sentence MY FREIGHT TRAIN IS _____. A graphic of a train can be generated from Kid Pix by using the Stamps option and enlarging the graphic to create a form for the students to complete as they decide what word to use.
2. The teacher schedules computer lab time with the library media specialist. Students are given instruction by the library media specialist in using the paint bucket tool, color choices, and text

tool in Kid Pix. Students are allowed time to practice using these tools.

3. The students color in the various areas of their train (in the Kid Pix program) with the paint bucket tool, paint a background, and use the text tool to put their names on the screen and to complete the sentence above with the word they have chosen. Scanned or digitized camera images can be added for each child if time allows.

4. The library media specialist will save the screens; using the slide show feature of Kid Pix, assemble into a slide show. The students will return to the media center to record their voices while reading their sentence.

SECTION B:

SAMPLE LESSONS INTEGRATING INFORMATION SKILLS INTO THE SCIENCE CURRICULUM

11. Minibeast Homes
12. Butterflies
13. Birthstones
14. Levers and Pulleys in Daily Life
15. Eye Disorders

11 MINIBEAST HOMES

AUDIENCE
Second grade. The media specialist and teacher plan and team teach this activity in conjunction with a unit on habitats. If it is taught at the end of the science unit, it could become a performance assessment tool.

INSTRUCTIONAL OBJECTIVE
This project is designed to provide opportunities for students to

1. explore the habitats of minibeasts.
2. begin to use reference tools such as *First Connections, Raintree Illustrated Science Encyclopedia*, or easy nonfiction books.

INFORMATION LITERACY OBJECTIVE

Locate Information
Begin to use print and electronic reference sources.

Process Information
Read and record information.

Create and Communicate Results
Produce a picture.

Assess Process and Product
Evaluate the process and product with the students.

ANTICIPATORY SET
During the unit on habitats, the media specialist and the teacher should meet to plan this activity. To begin the activity, the teacher or media specialist should tell students that they will be planning a minibeast zoo. Ask students to brainstorm what minibeasts to include in their zoo and what kinds of habitats the minibeasts will need. Then tell the students that they should each pick one minibeast and find out about its natural habitat. They should design homes for their minibeasts and draw and illustrate them on poster paper to put in a large display of the class insect zoo.

INSTRUCTIONAL INPUT/MODELING

After introducing the activity, instruct the students in how to use a simple science encyclopedia and *First Connections* to look up a minibeast. Show them how to record information using drawings and words. *First Connections* has a simple ABC search. Articles in *First Connections* on minibeasts include ants, bees, beetles, flies, grasshoppers, caterpillars, spiders, butterflies and moths, centipedes and millipedes, salamanders and newts, snails, spiders, and worms. Guide the students in finding and recording on the sheet provided information from the electronic encyclopedia and other appropriate sources about their minibeast.

Then students should draw and illustrate their minibeasts in their natural habitats on large drawing paper to attach to a large butcher paper strip for a class zoo display. Students could also make dioramas of their minibeast zoo exhibit.

CHECK FOR UNDERSTANDING/EVALUATION

Discuss with the students which sources they liked using and which were the most useful. Ask them what they learned about minibeasts and their habitats.

BIBLIOGRAPHY

First Connections: The Golden Book Encyclopedia. (CD ROM) San Diego: Josten's Learning, 1992.
Raintree Illustrated Science Encyclopedia. Austin, Tex.: Steck Vaughn, 1991.

To use a copy of the Minibeast Homes notetaking form:

1. Open the CD-ROM and go to the Chapter 11 Folder.
2. Click to open the Folder.
3. Scroll down to Minibeast Notetaking Form
4. Click to open.

MINIBEAST HOMES

Name of Minibeast:

Food and Water	Light, Air, and Space
Shelter	**Other Plants and Animals**

12 BUTTERFLIES

AUDIENCE

Second Grade. This activity may be used as part of a life cycle of butterflies unit. In this unit, students complete an activity sheet and give characteristics of insects by comparing their butterflies to spiders. The teacher and media specialist could team teach this activity after the students have completed a butterfly science unit.

INSTRUCTIONAL OBJECTIVE

1. Develop an understanding of the monarch butterfly.
2. Develop an awareness of the similarities and differences between butterflies and spiders

The main objective of one second grade science unit is for students to observe the painted-lady butterfly's life cycle. Learning about the life cycle of the monarch butterfly and comparing it to different kinds of spiders could be a meaningful extension of the unit.

INFORMATION LITERACY OBJECTIVE

Process the Information

Listen critically to information.
Compare and contrast information.

Create and Communicate Results

Synthesize information into a chart, story, or class book.

Assess Process and Product

Teacher or media specialist assesses the student products.
Students reflect on what they have learned.

ANTICIPATORY SET

After completing the science unit on butterflies, the teacher or media specialist should ask students what they know about the monarch butterfly and how it is different from a spider. They could also compare the monarch to the painted-lady butterfly. The teacher or media specialist could record the students' information on a chart.

INSTRUCTIONAL INPUT/MODELING

Read aloud both *Monarch Butterfly* and *Spiders* by Gail Gibbons. As you read, stop to ask students what they have learned and have them make comparisons between monarchs and spiders. Record their responses on a class chart. After both titles have been read, have the students compare and contrast monarchs and spiders, using the chart as a guide. Have the students suggest categories for their comparisons, such as food, shelter, life cycle, appearance, etc. Students could then make their own charts to display in the classroom or media center. Students could also write and illustrate butterfly and spider stories or create a class book or mural.

Other activities you can do with this unit are the following:

- Set up a monarch habitat in the classroom and record what happens on a class calendar. Students could also keep journals about their observations.
- Invite a volunteer from the Monarch Project to talk about the tagging process.
- If your school or community has a butterfly garden, the students could observe the butterflies that come to the garden. Bring several butterfly identification books so that students can identify the butterflies they see. Students and their families could also observe and identify butterflies in their own backyards and neighborhoods and could keep family journals of their observations.

BIBLIOGRAPHY

George, Jean Craighead. *The Moon of the Monarch Butterflies*. New York: HarperCollins, 1993.

Gibbons, Gail. *Monarch Butterfly*. New York: Holiday, 1989.

———. *Spiders*. New York: Holiday, 1993.

Heiberman, E. *The Great Butterfly Hunt*. New York: Simon & Schuster, 1990.

Lasky, Kathryn. *Monarchs*. New York: Harcourt, 1993.

Lavies, Bianca. *Monarch Butterflies: Mysterious Travelers*. New York: Dutton, 1993.

Mitchell, R. *Butterflies and Moths: A Golden Guide*. Racine, Wisc.: Golden, 1987.

Watts, B. *Butterflies and Moths, Keeping Minibeasts*. New York: Watts, 1991.

13 BIRTHSTONES

AUDIENCE

Fourth grade. As a short research project to accompany the earth materials unit in science, the students will learn about the properties of their own birthstones. They will communicate this data as an acrostic poster, using paper, pencil, and markers or using a word processor. This unit will provide opportunity for the students to practice notetaking and paraphrasing as well as creating a simple poster.

INSTRUCTIONAL OBJECTIVE

Develop an awareness of the properties of gemstones.

INFORMATION LITERACY OBJECTIVE

Define the Information Need

State the problem and the information requirements of the problem.

Locate Information

Brainstorm possible sources of information.
Evaluate which are the most useful.
Locate sources and information within sources.

Process the Information

Extract information by taking notes.

Create and Communicate Results

Make an acrostic to communicate information.

Assess Process and Product

The teacher or media specialist evaluates the products for accuracy, grammar, and punctuation. Students evaluate the information sources and determine which were the most useful.

ANTICIPATORY SET

The teacher or media specialist will tell the students that they will be doing research on their birthstones. The students take notes from reference sources and use their notes to make an illustrated acrostic about their birthstones. Ask the students what information about birthstones should be included in their notes. Suggestions may include color, hardness, where found, which country produces the most, and so forth. Then ask the students where to find information about birthstones.

Write their suggestions on the chalkboard and have them predict which sources will be the best.

INSTRUCTIONAL INPUT/MODELING

After the unit introduction, the media specialist teaches and models how to paraphrase and take notes. Emphasize to the students that they should put the information in their own words and that they should not use any words that they don't understand. After gathering their sources (trade books, a general encyclopedia, a science encyclopedia, a CD-ROM, etc.) the students should locate information about their birthstones, scan the information, and decide which sources are the best to use. Then they should read the information through quickly to decide which facts they should put in their notes. Then they should write their notes on paper, putting the information in their own words. Reading buddies can be assigned to students who need help.

The media specialist should model this process using quartz. Read parts of several sources aloud or show them on the overhead. Ask the students which sources would be the best to use. Include a printout on quartz from an electronic encyclopedia. After the best sources have been determined, read the article or section aloud several paragraphs at a time. Ask the students to pick out important facts and to restate the facts in their own words. Then copy their facts on the overhead. Continue this process until you have 10 to 15 facts recorded. (See sample notes.)

After modeling and checking for understanding, direct the students to gather material on their own birthstones, decide which sources to use, scan the material, and take notes. The media specialist or teacher should check each student's work. Go over each student's notes and make suggestions for improvement.

When most of the students have completed their notes, meet with the whole class to show them how to make a rough draft of an acrostic. On an overhead, write QUARTZ down the left side. Then tell the students that they have to think of descriptive phrases about quartz. Each phrase must begin with one of the letters of quartz. The first phrase should begin with Q. Model how to make a phrase for each letter before assigning students to do their own rough drafts.

Go over the rough draft with each student, checking for accuracy, spelling, and grammar. You could meet with the whole class during this process to show them a final product and to tell them that their acrostics should be illustrated with an original drawing. Students may use paper, pencil, and markers, or a word-processing program to make their final products.

CHECK FOR UNDERSTANDING/EVALUATION
The media specialist and the teacher evaluate each product for accuracy, spelling, and grammar.

The students discuss which sources were best for finding out about their birthstones.

BIBLIOGRAPHY

Podendorf, Illa. *Rocks and Minerals*. Chicago: Children's Press, 1988.
Raintree Illustrated Science Encyclopedia, 1991, s.v. "quartz."
Symes, R.F. *Rocks and Minerals*. New York: Knopf, 1988.

To use a copy of the Sample Notes for the Birthstones lesson:

1. Open the CD-ROM and go to the Chapter 13 Folder.
2. Click to open the Folder.
3. Scroll down to Birthstones Sample Notes.
4. Click to open.

To use the sample copy of a Birthstones project:

1. Open the CD-ROM and go to the Chapter 13 Folder.
2. Click to open the Folder.
3. Scroll to Birthstones Sample Project.
4. Click to open.

QUARTZ: SAMPLE NOTES

glossy mineral made of silicon and oxygen

found in granite and many other kinds of rock

pure quartz called rock crystal used to make jewelry

Amethyst is a purple-colored quartz.

Citrine is a golden-yellow quartz.

finest amethysts found in volcanic rock in India, Uruguay, and Brazil

kinds of quartz, jasper and flint, made up of many fine grains instead of large single crystals

used to make glass and lenses and in radios, tv, radar, and clocks

has hardness of 7 and is hard to scratch

Quartz crystals have six sides.

Birthstones Unit: Sample Project

(Students should find an illustration of their birthstone to add to the project).

Quite difficult to scratch, quartz has a hardness of 7.

Used in making glass, lenses, radios, tvs, and clocks

Amethyst is a purple colored quartz.

Rock crystal is pure quartz and is used to make jewelry.

To find quartz, look for crystals with six sides.

Zip to India, Uruguay, or Brazil to find the finest amethyst quartz.

14 LEVERS AND PULLEYS IN DAILY LIFE

AUDIENCE

Fifth grade. This activity can be taught in conjunction with a simple machines unit.

INSTRUCTIONAL OBJECTIVE

After developing an understanding of levers and pulleys in their science class, the students will investigate their historical and current role in helping people do their work. The students will develop an awareness of how a scientific principle can be applied to everyday life.

INFORMATION LITERACY OBJECTIVE

Define the Information Need

Identify the information requirements of the problem.

Locate Information

Determine the range of possible resources.
Evaluate the possible resources to determine which are the most useful.
Use library catalog and print and electronic sources.

Process the Information

Extract information from a source by scanning, paraphrasing, and notetaking.

Create and Communicate Results

Communicate information on a poster.
Demonstrate information to a class.

Assess Process and Product

Evaluate the process of finding, communicating, and demonstrating information.

ANTICIPATORY SET

The media specialist and teacher should meet to plan this activity as a culmination of the science unit on levers and pulleys. The media specialist and teacher may wish to brainstorm a list of key words beforehand in preparation for the student brainstorming activity. Students should have a good understanding of how levers and pulleys work before beginning this activity.

As an introduction to the unit, read aloud the following paragraph about Archimedes. Instruct the students that they will be finding out about machines that use levers and pulleys in the media center. Have them brainstorm about machines that might use levers and pulleys and where to find out about these machines and their inventors.

Passage to read aloud:

> Since ancient times, people have known that levers could help them with their work. An ancient Greek scientist, Archimedes (287–212 BC), was the first to explain how levers work. He is credited as saying, "Give me a place to stand and I will move the earth." He meant that if he had a lever that was long enough, he would be able to move earth by himself. This explanation was an important landmark in the development of science and technology because the same principle describes the inclined plane, gears and belts, pulleys and screws. He showed that by making observations and experimenting, it was possible to understand the basic principles of why things work the way they do. This project will help students understand how levers and pulleys have helped humans do their work.

INSTRUCTIONAL INPUT/MODELING

In the media center have students work in pairs to find as many machines that use levers and pulleys as they can and list them on a piece of paper. You may wish to have several copies of *The Way Things Work* as well as a copy of the CD-ROM version. Then meet as a whole class to make a master list of machines. Students may need to bring evidence to show that their contributions do use levers and pulleys before putting them on a master list. See bibliography for suggestions and sources to use.

Each student should choose one of the machines to research in depth and find out as much as they can about who invented the machine and when it was invented. They should gather information from various sources, scan the material, paraphrase it, and take notes. An excellent notetaking model is Barbara Jansen's "Reading for Information: Trash 'N Treasures" (see bibliography). The media specialist or teacher should help students as needed. After students have taken notes, the media specialist should model how to make an effective poster about a machine with a word processor or paper and pencil. The students can then give demonstration speeches about their machines. The posters could also be made into a class book.

CHECK FOR UNDERSTANDING/EVALUATION
The teacher, media specialist, and students should evaluate the process of finding information, note taking, making a poster, and giving a demonstration.

BIBLIOGRAPHY

Bender, Lionel. *Invention*. New York: Knopf, 1991.

Burnie, David. *Machines and How They Work*. New York: Dorling Kindersley, 1991.

Catherall, Ed. *Exploring Uses of Energy*. Austin, Tex.: Steck-Vaughn, 1991.

Horvatic, Anne. *Simple Machines*. New York: Dutton, 1989.

How Things Work. [Washington, D.C.]: National Geographic Society, 1983.

Jansen, Barbara. "Reading for Information: The Trash-N-Treasure Method." *School Library Media Activities Monthly* 12 (February 12, 1996): pp. 29–32.

Lampton, C. *Seesaws, Nutcrackers, Brooms: Simple Machines That Are Really Levers*. Brookfield, Conn.: Millbrook, 1991.

Macaulay, David. *The Way Things Work*. Boston: Houghton, 1988.

Macaulay, David. *The Way Things Work CD-ROM*. New York: Dorling Kindersley, 1994.

Smithsonian Visual Timeline of Inventions: From the First Stone Tools to Satellites and Superconductors. London, New York: Dorling Kindersley, 1994.

To use the page of examples of levers and pulleys:

1. Open the CD-ROM and go to the Chapter 14 Folder.
2. Click to open the Folder.
3. Scroll down to Examples of Levers and Pulleys.
4. Click to open.

Examples of Levers and Pulleys

First-class levers
Seesaw
Balance
Nail extractor
Pliers (compound lever)
Scissors (compound lever)

Second-class levers
Wheelbarrow
Door
Bottle opener
Nutcracker

Third-class levers
Golf club
Hammer
Fishing pole
Tweezers

Multiple levers
Excavator
Nail clipper
Piano
Manual typewriter

Pulleys
Chain hoist
Block and tackle
Fork lift
Crane
Escalator
Elevator
Fan belt and crankshaft in a car
Bicycle crankshaft and chain drive

15 EYE DISORDERS

AUDIENCE

Sixth grade (Prerequisite: Completed a sight and sound unit or have incorporated sight into an optics unit.)

INSTRUCTIONAL OBJECTIVE

This project is designed to provide an opportunity for students to

1. learn about the human eye, its disorders, and corrective lenses.
2. survey a population.
3. communicate information effectively and accurately.
4. develop an awareness of the scientific process of gathering and recording information and making predictions.

INFORMATION LITERACY OBJECTIVE

Define the Information Need

Define the problem, the information requirements, and possible formats for the product.

Locate Information

Develop a research plan.
Identify and survey a population

Process the Information

Record information with a survey.

Create and Communicate Results

Synthesize information using a graph or database.
Produce an oral presentation.

Assess Process and Product

Evaluate the process.
Evaluate the results.

ANTICIPATORY SET

As a culmination activity for a sight and sound unit or after having incorporated sight as part of an optics unit, the teacher and media specialist should meet to plan this activity. They may introduce the activity by presenting the following scenario:

Researchers working with the human eye are experimenting with new kinds of lenses to correct common eye disorders. In order to conduct their research, the scientists need to know which kinds of eye disorders are most common in adults and children.

Brainstorm with the students to determine how to find out the common eye disorders and how to take a sampling of children and adults to find out what percentage of children and adults have eye disorders and what those disorders are. These samplings could extend to other schools by sending the survey to selected teachers, schools, and administrators in the district via e-mail.

INSTRUCTIONAL INPUT/MODELING

With input from the students, set up a survey form for gathering data that includes adults and children and common eye problems such as near-sightedness, far-sightedness, astigmatism, cataracts, and others. Determine the number of children and adults each student should survey. Each student then gathers data, using the survey form.

Each student puts his or her survey results on a graph, using Microsoft Word or another program with graphing capabilities. Students will meet with the media specialist for instruction on how to use Word to make a graph.

When the students have completed their graphs, assign a team of experts to put all the information on one graph or database. Then have the team show the results to the entire class to identify common eye problems and the percentage of the surveyed population who have eye problems. Teams could also research the common eye problems and present their findings to the class.

CHECK FOR UNDERSTANDING/EVALUATION

Discuss the process of surveying and making a graph or a database with the students. Discuss the accuracy of the results

TO CREATE A GRAPH USING MICROSOFT WORD

Step One: Open the Graph program

1. Open Microsoft Word
2. Find the graph button in the ruler (looks like bar graph) and click once.
3. You will see a small spreadsheet and a graph.
4. Click in the title box of the graph and drag it to the lower half of your page so that you can see both the spreadsheet and the graph.

Step Two: Type the information into the spreadsheet.

1. Select all of the contents of the spreadsheet and use the Edit menu to clear all.
2. Type the names of the eye disorders in the boxes across the top line of the spreadsheet. (Do not type anything in the upper left-hand box.)
3. Type "Child," "Adult," "Male," "Female," or other categories in the boxes on the far left-hand column of the chart. Do not type in the upper left-hand corner box.
4. Fill in your data from the survey in the proper cells in the spreadsheet (see illustration: Creating a Graph).
5. A chart symbol next to a row in the spreadsheet designates information that will be graphed, whether you have information typed in that row/column or not. Be sure Word is only graphing rows and columns in which you have typed information. Clear any "extras."

Step Three: Fixing Up Your Graph

1. Go to Format—Chart Type and select the kind of graph you want.
2. If your graph does not contain the data you want, go to the Data menu and change to Series in Rows.
3. The Insert menu will give you different options to get titles and a legend.

Step 4: Saving and Printing Your Graph

1. Go to File, pull down to Update.
2. Go to File, pull down to "Quit and Return."
3. You will now be back in your Word document. Save the file and print.

To Return to the Graph That You Have Created

Double click in the middle of the graph in your WORD document, and the graph program will reappear.

The directions for creating a graph using Microsoft Word are on the CD-ROM. To use them:

1. Open the CD-ROM and go to the Chapter 15 Folder.
2. Click to open the Folder.
3. Scroll down to Create a Graph Using Microsoft Word Form
4. Click to open.

Creating a Graph

Decide by looking at your data what headings you want. Click the box, type the title and hit Tab to move to the next cell.

This box should always remain blank

Child - M				
Adult - M				
Child - F				

Enter your survey groups here

Type the numbers you want in each cell

SECTION C:

SAMPLE LESSONS INTEGRATING INFORMATION SKILLS INTO THE SOCIAL STUDIES CURRICULUM

16 TRAVEL BROCHURES

AUDIENCE

Fourth Grade. Students will create a travel brochure for a state or region of the United States using paper and pencil or a word processor.

INSTRUCTIONAL OBJECTIVE

The purpose of this unit is to give students an opportunity to synthesize information about a state or region of the United States.

1. The student will learn how to organize a presearch on a given topic.
2. The student will organize information into a logical format to produce a travel brochure.

INFORMATION LITERACY OBJECTIVES

Define the Information Need

Identifies the information requirements of the problem by brainstorming which types of information to put in a travel brochure.

Locate Information

Organizes a presearch, looking for key words and phrases, descriptions, and headings. Locates and evaluates materials on a state or region of the United States.

Process the Information

Takes notes on a state or region of the United States.

Create and Communicate Results

Organizes information into a travel brochure and finds or makes visuals to illustrate it.

Assess Process and Product

Evaluates own brochure and a brochure of a classmate, using the form provided.

ANTICIPATORY SET

The teacher or media specialist will introduce the activity by showing several commercial travel brochures from various states. Ask the students what makes a good travel brochure and what techniques can be used to make a brochure attractive. Then tell the students that they are going to make travel brochures for a state or region of the United States using paper and pencil, a word processor or a combination of these. After states or regions have been assigned, model the presearch strategies using the prepared transparency on Iowa (My Search) as follows:

INSTRUCTIONAL INPUT/MODELING

The media specialist will share the pathfinder for the media center and discuss sources specific to the states or regions being studied (see Sample Elementary Pathfinder on page 269). The teacher or media specialist will then discuss the presearch methods of stating the problem, choosing key words to look up in a source, and choosing possible sources to examine.

The students do a presearch guide on their states or regions using the blank form included in the unit and discuss their guides with the teacher or media specialist. After the discussions the students make appropriate additions and deletions.

The students will then take notes on their state or region and will make rough drafts of their travel brochures. After completing the rough drafts, the students will meet with the teacher or media specialist to proof their brochures and plan appropriate visuals. The final copy may be done by hand or on the computer. The media specialist will teach techniques necessary to prepare the brochure on the computer.

CHECK FOR UNDERSTANDING/EVALUATION

Students discuss which sources were the best. Students evaluate their own brochures and a classmate's brochure, using the form provided.

To use completed My Search Form as well as a form template and the Travel Brochure Evaluation on CD-ROM:

1. Open the CD-ROM and go to the Chapter 16 Folder.
2. Click to open the Folder.
3. Scroll down to Travel Brochure documents.
4. Click to open.

My Search

RESEARCH PROBLEM	What would tourists like to see in Iowa?
KEY WORDS	Iowa, Agriculutre, Mesquaki Des Moines, Mississippi River, Loess Hills, Herbert Hoover, Midwest
LARGER SUBJECTS	Midwest, Agriculture, Mississippi River
NARROWER SUBJECTS	Des Moines, Mesquaki, Herbert Hoover, Loess Hills
SOURCES TO EXAMINE	*World Book*, *Encarta*, *Groliers*, *America Alive*, nonfiction books from the general collection, prepared brochures and pamphlets

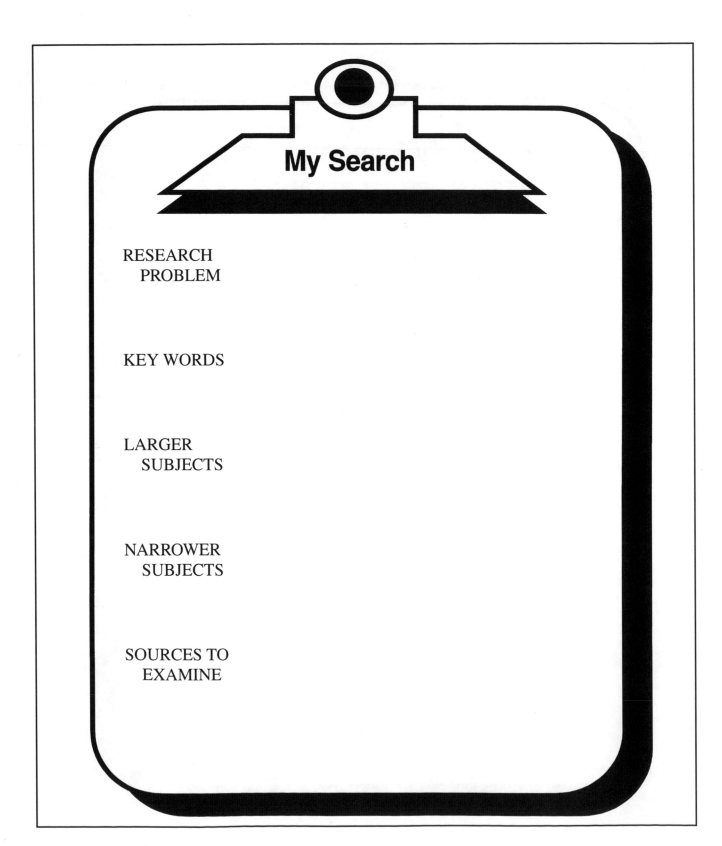

My Search

RESEARCH
  PROBLEM

KEY WORDS

LARGER
  SUBJECTS

NARROWER
  SUBJECTS

SOURCES TO
  EXAMINE

Travel Brochure Evaluation

Evaluate the brochure, using these ratings:

1.	2.	3.
excellent	**good**	**needs improvement**

_____ Facts are accurate and interesting

_____ Visuals are attractive and appropriate

_____ Overall rating

Comments and suggestions for improvement:

Student's Name_____ Evaluator's Name_____

'17 PEOPLE OF THE AMERICAN REVOLUTION

AUDIENCE

Fifth grade (U.S. History). As a research project to accompany the study of the Revolutionary War period of American History, students will research the life and times of notable people who lived then.

INSTRUCTIONAL OBJECTIVE

Students will develop an awareness of contributions of significant people from the time of the American Revolution.

INFORMATION LITERACY OBJECTIVE

Define the Information Need

Brainstorm what information to find out about contributors to our history. Teacher will provide list of names (see page 179).

Locate Information

List places to look for information.
Use library catalog to locate biography and nonfiction trade books.
Review use of index and table of contents in selected books.

Process the Information

Media specialist will introduce *Webster's Biographical Dictionary* or *American Biography.*

Create and Communicate Results

Student pairs will create a part of a magazine of the past modeled on *Time* or *People.*

Assess Process and Product

Self-evaluation and parent-evaluation of project.

INSTRUCTIONAL INPUT/MODELING

From the list of famous Revolutionary War figures, each student will select or be assigned one on whom to do research. The class will brainstorm what facts should be included in a magazine article about that person based upon their own knowledge of what is in popular magazines such as *Time, Newsweek* or *People.*

The media specialist will introduce biographical sources to the students and explain that they are very valuable for this type of research. The class will discuss other good places to find information about a person. Each student will take notes on the assigned person's contribution and determine a way to share what the person is known for in our history. In creating their magazines they might consider including a letter to the editor, feature articles, cartoons, or obituaries. The items will be collated into magazine format and shared with all class members.

ASSESS PROCESS AND PRODUCT

Students will develop a rubric to evaluate the magazine. They will do it in pairs and then share their work with the whole class. The magazine will be shared by having parents evaluate it using the same rubric.

The list of Revolutionary War Period Figures is located on the CD-ROM should you wish to add or delete names. To use it:

1. Open the CD-ROM and go to the Chapter 17 Folder.
2. Click to open the Folder.
3. Scroll down to Revolutionary Figures List.
4. Click to open.

Revolutionary War Period Figures

Adams, Abigail
Adams, John
Adams, Samuel
Allen, Ethan
Arnold, Benedict
Attucks, Crispus
Banneker, Benjamin
Braddock, Edward
Brant, Joseph
Burgoyne, John
Burr, Aaron
Cornwallis, Lord Charles
de Grasse, Count
Equiano, Olaudah (Gustavus Vassa)
Forten, James
Franklin, Benjamin
George III, King
Greene, Gen. Nathan
Hale, Nathan
Hamilton, Alexander
Hancock, John
Henry, Patrick
Howe, Gen. Sir William

Jefferson, Thomas
Jones, John Paul
Jouett, Jack
Lafayette, Marquis de
Madison, James
Marion, Francis
Monroe, James
Ontacette
Paine, Thomas
Pinckney, Eliza Lucas
Pitcher, Molly
Pulaski, Count
Revere, Paul
Rochambeau, Comte de
Ross, Betsy
Sampson, Deborah
Sherburne, Andrew
Steuben, Baron Friedrich von
Warren, Mercy Otis
Washington, George
Wheatley, Phyllis
Zenger, Peter

Developed by Alice Kurtz, Weber Elementary School, Iowa City, Iowa

PART III:
MODEL LESSONS AND UNITS FOR SECONDARY CLASSES

18 INFORMATION PROBLEM SOLVING: INTRODUCTORY LESSON

The following is a script for an instructional activity including a lecture with accompanying note-taking guide, question and answer sheet, transparencies for recording responses, and reinforcement of key concepts. Modeling and checks for understanding are incorporated.

AUDIENCE
Seventh grade. This can be taught as part of a series of information literacy lessons taught in conjunction with language arts classes or incorporated as part of a research unit in a core curricular area.

INSTRUCTIONAL OBJECTIVES
1. The learner will gain an understanding of the information problem-solving process.
2. The learner will identify appropriate sources to meet an information need.
3. The learner will identify appropriate tools for information location and access.
4. The learner will evaluate sources of information using specified criteria.

INFORMATION LITERACY OBJECTIVES

Define the Information Need
Define the problem to be solved

Locate Information
Determine the range of possible resources, assessing which are most useful
Locate sources
Find information within sources
Select appropriate resources

ANTICIPATORY SET
In daily life, the need for information arises constantly. When this happens, there are steps you can follow to solve your information problem. The first thing you should do is determine exactly **what you need**

to know. What problem must you solve? What questions must you answer? This stage is called define the information need. If you are clear about your information needs, finding the answers will be much easier. (Distribute note-taking form).

The next step is to locate information. You should think about where the information you need might be located. Determine the possible resources that could help and decide which would be *most* useful. Different types of resources are useful for different information needs. Now you are ready to actually find the information you need. To do this, you must locate the source that contains the information. You must also locate the information *within* the source. Today we will take a look at common information problems and go through steps 1 and 2. Learning how to attack an information problem will help you both in daily life and in school. The purpose of today's lesson is to show you what to do when you have an information need.

INSTRUCTIONAL INPUT / MODELING

Scenario One—You are considering going to a movie on Saturday. Model Defining the Information Need by having students brainstorm about the problem to be solved. Record responses using Problem-Solving Model on pages 192–193. Suggested responses are listed below.

Step 1:Define the Information Need—What do you need to know? (*What movies are showing? Which theater? What times? Do you have enough money? What is your schedule for Saturday? Transportation? Which movie is the best? If you plan to go with a friend, is the friend available and interested?*)

Step 2: Locate Information—Where are the answers located?

- What movies are showing? Where? When? (*newspaper; call theaters, etc.*) The newspaper and the theater are called sources of information.
- What source(s) could help you decide which showing best fits into your schedule on Saturday? (*a calendar; a parent, etc.*)
- What source(s) could you consult to determine your transportation? (*parent; older brother or sister; bus schedule, etc.*)
- What source(s) could help you find out which movie is the best one to see? (*movie ratings in the newspaper; movie reviews in a newspaper or magazine; online movie review services; a friend who has seen a particular movie, etc.*)
- What source will tell you if your friend wants to go with you? (*the friend*)

Show transparency on page 194, Sources of Information, to review different types of sources of information. Discuss the following:

- A source can be printed information such as a newspaper or magazine.
- A source can be a very specialized reference such as a bus schedule or calendar.
- A source can be an expert or knowledgeable individual such as a parent, brother, sister, movie reviewer, or friend.
- A source can be outside the resources you have at hand, such as the theater itself.

Evaluation of Sources

Often the information you need can be found in more than one source. You should determine which source(s) would be most useful. You do this by examining advantages and disadvantages. (Which source(s) would be most useful?)

Which source would be the best for finding out what movies are showing where and when—the newspaper or the theaters themselves?

Newspaper Advantages: All movie information is listed in one place; can compare locations and times easily; easy access to lots of information.

Newspaper Disadvantages: It may not be available (you do not subscribe to the paper; not able to find it because it is under a bed somewhere in the house; got rained on, and so forth); the information may be out-dated if the paper is not current and the movies in town have changed.

Theater Advantages: The information may be more reliable and current; may provide additional information such as price, what time the movie gets over if you need someone to pick you up, directions to the theater if you do not know where it is located.

Theater Disadvantages: Information is more difficult to access because you need a phone book; the line may be busy; you may need to call several theaters to compare information.

Which source would be best for determining which showing would fit into your Saturday schedule—a calendar or a parent?

Calendar Advantages: At your house everything is written down on a calendar so the information is easily available and reliable.

Calendar Disadvantages: At your house the calendar is not kept up-to-date so something could conflict with the movie but it is not written down; your father's handwriting is illegible—if you cannot read what he wrote on the calendar this source is unusable.

Parent Advantages: Your mother always knows the family schedule so her information is reliable; she is the "authority."

Parent Disadvantages: Your mother is not home, so the information is not available.

When deciding which source of information is the best, there are seven criteria to use to evaluate each source. (Show Evaluation of Sources on page 195).

1. Appropriateness
   Does it have the type and amount of information I need?

2. Availability
   Is the source readily available?
   Is the information easy to access?

3. Relevance
   Is information from this source pertinent to my need?

4. Suitability
   Can I use this source?
   Am I able to locate information in the source?
   Can I read or understand the information from this source?

5. Currency
   Is it important that the information be up-to-date?
   If so, is it current enough to be accurate and useful?

6. Authority
   Was the information prepared by an expert or knowledgeable individual(s)?
   Is this individual qualified to write or speak on this topic?
   Does the person know what he/she is talking about?

7. Reliability
   Is the information factual or is it just opinion?
   Can the information be backed up by other sources?

Apply the seven criteria for evaluating sources to these information needs:

- Which source would be the best in determining your transportation to the movie—a parent, sibling, or bus schedule?
- Which source would be the most useful in determining which movie to see—ratings in the newspaper, movie reviews in a newspaper or magazine, online movie reviews, a friend?

Return to the Problem-Solving Model to record responses.

Locate the source and *the information within the source.*
Once you have applied the criteria and decided which source would be the best, you must locate that source. You must also locate the information *within* the source. Sometimes this is easy; sometimes it is more difficult. Let's look at the sources we have considered for our information need and talk about location and access.

- Sources for finding what movies are showing, when, and where: (*theater or newspaper*)

  If you call the theater, someone there can answer your questions about the movie, so the theater itself can be a source of information. To call the theater, however, you need a tool. What tool do you need? (*phone book*) A tool is something that helps you locate a source of information. Show the Tools transparency (page 196).

  If you use the newspaper, you may need a tool to help you find the movie section. What tool could you use? (*index on the front page*) A tool can be something that helps you access information within a source.

Using Problem-Solving Model to record responses, discuss the following:

- Sources for determining which showing fits into your schedule: (*calendar or parent*)

  Do you need any special tool to help you access information from a calendar? (*No*) Not every source requires a tool to help you locate and access information. A source like a calendar is one you can just open up and find out what you need to know very easily.

  Do you need any special tool to help you get information from a parent? (*Probably not, unless your parent is not at home and you must look up a number in a phone book or other directory to be able to reach him or her.*)

- Sources to help you determine transportation (*parent, brother or sister, bus schedule*)

  Do you need a tool to get information from a parent or sibling? (*No*)

  Assume that you have a bus schedule handy at your house. Do you need a tool to help you access information within the schedule? (*If the schedule uses special symbols or abbreviations, you may need a key to help you interpret the information.*)

- Sources to help you decide which movie is the best: (*movie ratings in the newspaper, movie reviews in the newspaper or a magazine, a friend who has seen a particular movie*)

What tool could you use to help you find movie ratings or reviews in the newspaper? (*index*)

Would you need a tool to help you locate a movie review in a magazine? (*It depends—if you know there is a review in a current magazine that you have available, you may not need anything except the table of contents in that issue. If you are not sure where a review is located, you need a special tool to help you locate the source of information about the movie.*)

There are special tools designed to help you locate magazine articles. One such tool is a paper index called *Readers' Guide to Periodical Literature.* Another tool which is even easier to use is an electronic index to magazines called *Magazine Article Summaries*, or *MAS*. You could use *MAS* to type in the name of a movie or key words related to the movie. This tool would help you locate articles about the movie and would include the name of the magazine in which the article or review appeared. It would also tell you the date of the magazine, the page number, the length of the article, perhaps who wrote the article, if there were pictures, etc. You will learn more about how to use *MAS* in another lesson.

A tool like *MAS* can be very useful, but only when it is available. You probably wouldn't have *MAS* at home so you would have to locate the article at school. This is more work than looking in the newspaper or calling a friend. When you are deciding which source of information is the most useful, sometimes you also have to consider the tools you need. A movie review in a magazine might be more reliable or authoritative, but not as available as other sources.

- If you wanted to know what a friend thought of the movie or if the friend was interested in going to the movie with you, what source would you need to locate? (*friend*).

What tool might you need to locate that source of information?

(If you didn't know the friend's phone number, you might need a phone book or school directory.)

Review tools using the information on III—Tools transparency, page 196.

- A tool to help you locate a source could be a phone book or other directory.

- A tool to help you locate a source could be a special index like *Readers' Guide to Periodical Literature* or *Magazine Article Summaries (MAS)*.

- A tool to help you access information within a source could be an index or a special key.

The criteria you use to determine the best source of information can also be used to evaluate the tools you may need to use with those sources. Show transparency on Evaluation of Sources. Apply this criteria to the tools of a phone book and school directory.

Information Literacy Model Continued

We have discussed the first two stages in the information problem-solving process. There are actually five stages. We will look at steps 3–5 briefly. Return to Problem-Solving Model. Look at Step 3: Processing Information. Explain the concept of extracting information from a source. How would you extract information from the various sources? *(read, listen, take notes, and so forth.)*

Look at Step 4: Create and Communicate Results. During this step you use the information you have gathered to finish the job—create, produce, communicate, or present what you have learned. Using our movie scenario, what would happen at this point in the information problem-solving process? *(You would make a decision about what movie to see, when, where, transportation, and communicate that decision to parents, friend, etc. Go to the movie.)*

Look at Step 5: Assess the Process and the Product. How would you assess the product? *(Did you make a good decision? Did you enjoy the movie?)* How would you assess the process? *(Did you find the information you needed efficiently? What would you do differently next time?)*

GUIDED PRACTICE

We have just gone through the five steps in the information problem-solving process. The scenario we discussed involved a common information problem. Many information problems arise from school work. Let's practice the process using a different information problem.

Scenario Two—**You are doing your math homework, which is an end-of-the chapter review, when you come across a word you do not understand. If you do not find out what the word means, you will not be able to complete the assignment and you will probably not do well on the test tomorrow.**

The media specialist will then lead the class through the information problem-solving process, emphasizing defining the problem and locating information (sources of information, tools, and evaluation of sources.)

INDEPENDENT PRACTICE

In small groups, students will practice information problem solving. Each group will be given a transparency copy of the model. The group will be given at least one scenario representing an information problem to work through. If time permits, one scenario could be a real-life situation, the other school related. Results and responses should be recorded on the transparency. When the exercise is completed, groups will share their responses.

SUGGESTED SCENARIOS

You want to buy something (such as a bike, CD player, computer software).

You are going to plan a party.

Your family is planning a vacation or trip.

You are planning your class schedule for next year.

A friend recommended a TV show to you but you forgot when it is on.

You need to know how to spell a word.

You need to find some geographical information (the location of a country, a capital, a river).

Other examples should reflect typical school information situations.

To use the transparencies for the Information Problem-Solving Introductory Lesson, the Follow-Up Lesson, on CD-ROM:

1. Open the CD–ROM and go to the Chapter 19 Folder.
2. Scroll to the item you want.
3. Click to open.

To use the activity sheet and Note-Taking Guide, repeat the process above, but open the Activity Sheet folder and select Sources and Tools Activity. You may also want to use the Seven Quick Ways to Evaluate Information bookmark with this activity. This is located in the folder labeled Chapter 3.

Information Problem Solving: Note-taking Guide

1. Step 1 in solving an information problem is _____ .
   Key question: _____ .

2. Step 2 is to _____ .

3. Next you decide which_____ would be most useful.

4. The seven criteria for evaluating sources are:

   - _____   - _____
   - _____   - _____
   - _____   - _____
                    - _____

5. During Step 2 of information problem solving, you_____
   the sources and _____ information within the source.

6. For location, you sometimes need to use _____ .

7. During Step 3, you _____ information from a source.

8. During Step 4, you _____ a product which helps you
   to _____ the information you have learned.

9. Step 5 in information problem solving is to evaluate the_____
   you created and how efficiently you went through the _____ .

Information Problem-Solving Model

Step 1: Define the Information Need

(What do you need to know?)

Step 2: Locate Information

(Where are the answers located?)

(Which sources would be the most useful?)

(Where can you find the needed resources?)

(What tools do you need to access the information?)

Information Problem-Solving Model

Step 3: Process the Information

Step 4: Create and Communicate Results

Step 5: Assess the Process and Product

Information Problem Solving

Sources of Information

A source is where information can be found.

Different sources fit different information needs.

✔ **A source can be printed information such as a newspaper or magazine.**

✔ **A source can be a very specialized reference such as a bus schedule or calendar.**

✔ **A source can be an expert or knowledgeable individual such as a parent, brother, sister, movie reviewer, or friend.**

✔ **A source can be outside the resources you have at hand such as the theater itself.**

Information Problem Solving

Evaluation of Sources

✔ **Appropriateness:**

Does it have the type and amount of information I need?

✔ **Availability:**

Is the source readily available? Is the information easy to access?

✔ **Relevance:**

Is the information from this source pertinent to my need?

✔ **Suitability:**

Am I able to locate information in the source? Can I read or understand the information?

✔ **Currency:**

Is it important that the information be up-to-date? Is it current enough to be accurate and useful?

✔ **Authority:**

Was the information prepared by an expert or knowledgeable individual(s)? Is this individual qualified to write or speak on this topic?

✔ **Reliability:**

Is the information factual or is it just opinion?

Can it be backed up by other sources?

Information Problem Solving

Tools for Locating Information

A tool can be used to help locate a source of information.
A tool can be used to access information within a source.

✔ **A tool to help you locate a source could be a phone book or other directory.**

✔ **A tool to help you locate a source could be a special index like the *Readers' Guide to Periodical Literature* or *Magazine Article Summaries* (*MAS*).**

✔ **A tool to help you access information within a source could be an index or a special key.**

19 INFORMATION PROBLEM SOLVING: FOLLOW-UP LESSON

AUDIENCE

Seventh grade. This can be taught as part of a series of information literacy lessons taught in conjunction with language arts classes or incorporated as part of a research unit in a core curricular area.

INSTRUCTIONAL OBJECTIVES

1. The learner will gain an understanding of the information problem-solving process.
2. The learner will identify appropriate sources to meet an information need.
3. The learner will identify appropriate tools for information location and access.
4. The learner will evaluate sources of information using specified criteria.

INFORMATION LITERACY OBJECTIVES

Define the Information Need

Define the problem

Locate Information

Determine the range of possible resources, assessing which are most useful
Locate sources
Find information within sources
Select appropriate resources

ANTICIPATORY SET

In our last lesson, you were introduced to the steps in the information problem-solving process. Let's quickly review what you learned, referring to your Note-Taking Guide, if necessary.

What is Step 1 called? (*Define the information need*) What is a key question you ask yourself during this step? (*What do I need to know?*) Remember, if you are clear about your information needs, finding the answers will be much easier. What happens during Step 2 of Locating Information? (*You develop a research plan.*) What is a key question you ask yourself during this step? (*Where are the answers located?*) During this step you determine the possible resources that might have the information you need and decide which would be *most* useful. What happens next? (*You locate the source that contains the information you need. You also access the information within the source.*) Review the terms source and tool using the relevant transparencies from Lesson 1, if desired.

In our last lesson we practiced information problem solving using some common situations or scenarios. Today we will practice Steps 1 and 2 with situations related to the kind of research you might have to do in school.

INSTRUCTIONAL INPUT / MODELING / CHECK FOR UNDERSTANDING

The purpose of today's lesson is to show you what to do when you have an information need that requires using the resources in the library media center. We will talk about developing a search strategy using the various sources and tools we have available here at [name of school].

The media specialist presents various scenarios and guides students through information problem solving, highlighting sources and tools available in that media center. Responses can be recorded on transparencies from Chapter 18. Examples should be relevant to that curriculum of the content area in which the instruction is taking place. The following scenarios are intended to serve as samples which can be adapted as needed.

Scenario One—Your social studies teacher has given you a map and told you to label various geographical locations. What do you do now?

Step 1: Define the Information Need

Step 2: Locate Information (Where can you find the answers?)

Discussion should include such sources as the textbook, atlas, general encyclopedia, specialized geographical references, appropriate CD-ROMs, books in the general collection, and other sources.

(Which sources would be the most useful?)

(Evaluate sources using the criteria for evaluation of sources (pages 39–42). The media specialist emphasizes that electronic sources such as CD-ROMs or the Internet are not necessarily the best source in all cases; format is only one consideration. Where can you find the resources you need? Focus on the physical location and arrangement of sources.

Next discuss which tools you need to access the information. (Review the two uses of tools using the transparency from Chapter 18. Discussion should include such tools as the index in a textbook, atlas, and encyclopedia.)

What tool would you use to locate a book in the general collection that might have a map you could use? (Explain the function of the library catalog as a location tool.) You will learn more about how to use the library catalog in another lesson. What tool would you use to access information from a CD-ROM or other electronic source? (Explain that such sources generally have a search screen that acts as a tool for access.)

Scenario Two—**Your social studies assignment is to find out the name of the money in a particular country (or insert name of a specific country if it has a curricular tie-in). You also need to find out the exchange rate in U.S. dollars. What do you do now?**

(Follow procedure in Scenario One. Focus on the almanac as a source for brief, current information. Discuss the appropriate use of the comprehensive and quick index as access tools.)

Scenario Three—**A teacher has assigned each student in the class to research a famous person.**

(This can be adapted for other subjects: history, music, art, literature, foreign language, science, math. Defining the information need should focus on the amount of information required. Discussion of sources should include general encyclopedias, biographical dictionaries, other relevant biographical reference sources, and individual and collective biographies. Focus on the evaluation of sources and appropriate tools such as indexes and the library catalog.)

Scenario Four—**A teacher has assigned you to read a recent article on a topic related to class. (In science, it could be a natural disaster, epidemic, or discovery. In math, it could be related to finance. In social studies, it could pertain to a region of the world or international relations.) What do you do now?**

(Focus on sources of current information, such as periodicals. Review tools for access to periodicals from Chapter 18. If appropriate, introduce other available sources such as *SIRS*, *NewsBank*, Vertical File, World Wide Web, or other outside sources.)

Scenario Five—**In science class each student selected an endangered animal from a list. Now you have to find out the following information: where the animal lives, why it is endangered, and what is being done to try to protect it. What do you do now?**

(In Defining the Information Need, you should focus on the amount of information needed and the format of the end product. Discussion of sources should include general encyclopedias, specialized science and environmental reference sources, pertinent CD-ROMs, the Internet, the general collection, and periodicals. Include evaluation of sources and appropriate tools.)

Scenario Six—In language arts class you are planning a debate on a current topic of local interest (such as an upcoming school bond issue, transformation to middle schools, in-district transfers, a tax hike, a zoning issue, the building of a controversial facility of some type). You need to gather some information to support your point of view. What do you do now?

(Focus on knowledgeable individuals as a source of information. The phone book or e-mail via Internet can be included as appropriate tools for location and access.)

Scenario Seven—For science class you must give a three-minute oral presentation on a specific disease, including the cause, prevention, and treatment. What do you do now?

(Defining the information need should include both the information need and format of the end product. Review appropriate sources and tools.)

Scenario Eight—You have to write a five-page report on a topic of your choice. You have no study halls or time to do this assignment at school. What do you do now?

(Follow the procedure in Scenario One. Focus on outside sources such as public or university libraries and their access tools.)

GUIDED PRACTICE

We have just practiced two steps in the information problem-solving process. In each scenario we had to determine the range of possible resources and assess which sources would be the most useful. This helps the students develop a research plan. Show Transparency III-5—Search Strategy Guide. For each source, ask students to identify appropriate tools for location and access. Note: This transparency will need revision to reflect the sources and tools available in each library media center.

INDEPENDENT PRACTICE

Students will work in small groups to complete the Activity Sheet labeled Sources and Tools.

Information Problem Solving Follow-up Lesson
Search Strategy Guide

_____ **Reference Collection**

Use indexes to access information within general and specialized sources.

_____ **General Collection**

Use library catalog to locate print and nonprint sources in our collection.

_____ **Periodicals**

Use Magazine Article Summaries (MAS) *to locate magazine articles.*

_____ **SIRS**

Use the electronic or paper SIRS *index to locate articles on social issues.*

_____ **Internet**

Use a search engine or bookmarks provided to locate information.

_____ **Vertical File**

Use the folders in the vertical file for pamphlets or newspaper articles.

_____ **Knowledgeable Individuals**

Consider interviewing an expert as a source of information. Use a phone book or Internet to access such a source.

_____ **Outside Sources**

Consider other libraries or agencies, such as the public libraries or nearby college or university libraries. Follow the same search strategy with these collections: Check the reference collection. Check the general collection using the catalog. Check for periodical articles using Infotrac, Magazine Index, Newspaper Index, *or other indexing tools.*

Information Problem Solving: Sources and Tools

Name _____   Teacher/Period _____ / _____

Directions: Below is a list of sources in the library. For each information problem, choose the one source you feel would be the most useful. Write the number of the source on the line.

1. **general encyclopedia**
2. **magazine article**
3. **almanac**
4. **outside library or agency**
5. **atlas**

6. **book in the nonfiction collection**
7. **Internet**
8. **specialized reference book**
9. **CD-ROM encyclopedia**
10. **knowledgeable individual**

___ You need brief facts and statistics about a baseball record to win a bet with a friend.

___ You need information about an upcoming vote faced by the city council.

___ You need in-depth information about the Holocaust for a five-page history paper.

___ You need current information on the situation in Bosnia.

___ You need to write a paper on Martin Luther King as an effective speaker. It would be helpful to hear him deliver his famous "I Have a Dream" speech.

___ You need a detailed map of France.

___ You need the most up-to-date information about a volcano that just erupted in Mexico.

___ You need a general overview on the topic of electricity.

___ Your hobby is training horses, but the media center does not have much information.

___ You need more than *World Book* has on Mozart, but you don't need an entire biography.

Directions: To locate and access information from the sources above, you might need to use a tool. Match each tool below with an appropriate source by writing the number on the line.

_____ Library catalog   _____ Public library   _____ Index– back of book

_____ Search screen   _____ Quick Thumb Index   _____ Index

_____ *Magazine Article Summaries*   _____ Phone book   _____ World Wide Web

20 LIBRARY CATALOG

AUDIENCE
Seventh graders as part of a series of Information Literacy lessons taught in conjunction with language arts classes or incorporated as part of a research unit in a core curricular area.

INSTRUCTIONAL OBJECTIVES
The learner will gain an understanding of the library catalog as a location tool. The learner will search the library catalog to explore the effects of

1. key-word and key-phrase searching,
2. Boolean connectors,
3. truncation, and
4. narrowing and broadening a search with related terms.

The learner will evaluate the results of a search to determine their usefulness.

INFORMATION LITERACY OBJECTIVES

Locate Information
Locate sources
Scan, screen, and select appropriate resources

ANTICIPATORY SET
In previous lessons, we learned that information needs can be met with various sources. Some of these sources require the use of a special tool. What tool can be used to locate the print and nonprint sources in our media center? *(the catalog)*. The library catalog is an electronic database that contains the records for information sources in the collection. What print sources can be located using the library catalog? *(fiction books, nonfiction books, short story collections, biographies, paperback books, reference books, professional books, etc.)* What nonprint sources can be located? *(videos, CDs, CD-ROMs, computer software, kits, audio tapes, records, games, and so forth.)*

Where is the library catalog located? *(point out work stations)* In our media center we have computers that are linked together or networked for the purpose of locating information. This is our library network. At each computer work station, you will find several information tools. Today we will concentrate on one of those tools. The purpose of today's lesson is to show you how to use the library catalog to locate sources here at school. You will also learn some strategies for searching that can be used with other electronic sources. (Distribute note-taking form.)

INSTRUCTIONAL INPUT / MODELING / CHECK FOR UNDERSTANDING:

The following is a script for instructional input including a demonstration with accompanying note-taking guide and question and answer checks for understanding. Modeling is to be done using a large screen display to project the library catalog screen from the computer.

This script was designed for use with seventh grade students conducting research as part of the rivers project in science. It is intended as a sample that includes the basic operation of the library catalog as well as key concepts related to electronic searching. This demonstration should be adapted to fit the curriculum and resources of each media center.

(*Note*: While the lesson which follows was designed to be used with the Iowa City Community School District's Library Network, for which the catalog is the Winnebago Library Catalog (DOS version), the concepts would be usable with any electronic library catalog. Minor changes in the script to reflect differing screen designs and search terms and procedures may need to be made.)

Library Catalog Demo Script

1. At the Library Network Main Menu, select Library Catalog. Press Enter. This displays the key-word search screen. This is the tool you use when you need information about something. You have a topic in mind, but do not know any specific titles or authors to look for. You need this tool to locate information on your topic by finding the key words you enter within the record for each potentially useful source.

2. On the top line of the key-word search screen, enter the key word "rivers"; press Enter. *How many items were found?* Explain the columns for title, author, location, material type, and status. Notice that the call number column is not in order. Explain why sorting the list is useful in the location of sources. *How do you sort the list? (F9)*

3. Press Escape to return to the search screen. *What key clears the screen? (F5)*

4. Type river*. (Get * by holding shift key and hitting the key with number 8.) This is called truncation. It is a way to abbreviate a key word. It tells the computer that you want records that contain either the word river OR rivers. Enter. *How many items were found?* Sort the list. Truncating may add some titles you don't want, but it is a way to expand your search so you don't miss some good things.

5. Escape. Use F5 to clear the search screen. Try a more specific search. Type "*nile*" (no caps needed); Enter. *How many hits did you get?* Sometimes being more specific is good. Materials will

be more relevant to your topic (Nile), but you may overlook some good general materials on rivers that include the Nile. Escape. F5.

6. Now try a key phrase. Enter Nile River. *How many hits? Why?* When you enter a key phrase, it must appear in the record exactly as you typed it in. If the record just said *Nile, not Nile River,* it might not appear in the result list. If it said *Nile: Egypt's Great River,* it might not pick it up. (Sometimes key phrases can be too limiting.)

7. *What would make a more general search?* Try egipt. (Misspell) WARNING. May mean there are no materials on this topic. *What else could be wrong?* (Spelling matters!) Escape. Clear. Try again. Egypt. *How many hits?* Sort.

8. Not all records will display on one screen. You could hit down arrow key, but it is easier to use Page Down. Pg Dn to call # 962 FEI. Look at the complete record. *Who is the author? # of pages? Title? Copyright?*

9. Escape. F5. Let's say your topic is the Amazon River. At the search screen, type amazon river. *How many hits? Why?* (Too specific) *What could we try instead?* Try amazon. *Hits? What's even more general?* Try brazil. *Hits?*

10. In Library Catalog, it is usually best to be more general; then narrow, if needed.

11. Let's say your topic is the pollution of rivers. Start with a general search. Enter pollution. Sort. Select call # 363.7 GAY. Look at the full record. Review parts of the record. Emphasize the complete call # for location. Look at the subject headings. *What is this book about?* (Air pollution/ozone) *If my topic is water pollution, will this book be useful?* (No). Let's refine the search. Escape.

12. Leave pollution on the top line. Arrow down to the second line. Type water. Now the record must contain both pollution AND water. *How many hits? What effect did adding AND water have on the search?* (Narrowed the search; more specific; fewer hits) *Is the book* Ozone *still in the list?*

13. Look at the records for two books and compare. *Which would be the best source?* 301.3 AYL or 363.7 LAN? *Why?* In evaluation of sources consider the date, length or scope, note (if available), subject headings, illustrations (if needed), etc.

14. Look at the book by Nardo. *What is the title? Would this be useful? Why or not?*

15. Escape. F5. On the top line, enter water pollution. *How many hits? Why?* (Key phrases are more limiting.) If time, skim through records. *Which is best source? Why?*

16. Key-phrase searching is useful when two words together express

what you really want. Try acid rain. Then try acid AND rain. *Any effect?* Try greenhouse effect as a phrase and using Boolean AND. Any effect?

17. Escape. F5. On the top line, type ecology. *How many hits did we get?* Arrow down to the second line. Now type environment. If we leave the search like this, the record for the source must contain both of these key words. Another trick in searching is to change the connecting word known as the Boolean. We've been using AND as a connector. Now we will try the Boolean OR. To change it to OR, press F2. *What effect does OR have on the search?* (Broadens it; makes it more general; more hits.)

18. Try toxic OR hazardous waste. Sort. After you evaluate the results list, you can get a printout of the sources you feel will be useful. First you must delete any unwanted titles, such as fiction. Demonstrate this process. Press F10. Explain printer setup.

19. Return to last search. Look at complete record for 363.7 SZU. Point out the title, note, and subject headings. Explain that these are the three places the computer looks for search terms when you do key-word searching. Explain that when you do subject searching, the only place the computer looks for terms is the subject headings.

20. Escape. F5. *How do you go into the Regular Catalog?* F7. Do this. Remind students that the Regular Catalog is best for title or author searching. Demonstrate, if desired. Show the subject-searching prompt. Point out that you cannot combine terms with Boolean or truncate at this search screen. Emphasize the advantages of key word!

21. Return to key-word search screen. Demonstrate the Boolean BUT NOT. (Samples: Nile BUT NOT Kinnick; pollution BUT NOT air.) *What effect does this Boolean have?* (Narrows the search because it excludes some records.)

GUIDED PRACTICE

Students will work in small groups to complete the activity. The media specialist and teacher will check progress as the students practice searches.

INDEPENDENT PRACTICE

To be determined by the teacher or media specialist based on the curricular unit.

To access the activity sheet for the library catalog lesson:

1. Open the CD-ROM and go to the Chapter 20 Folder.
2. Click to open the Folder.
3. Scroll to the Catalog Activity Sheet.
4. Click to open.

There is also a note-taking guide to help students record and remember lesson input for this lesson on the CD-ROM. To use the note-taking guide:

1. Open the CD-ROM and go to the Chapter 20 Folder.
2. Click to open the Folder.
3. Scroll down to the Note-taking Guide.
4. Click to open.

Library Catalog Note-Taking Guide

1. The Library Catalog is a_____ to help you locate the print and nonprint _____ of information in the library.

2. The Library Catalog is a database that contains the_____ for each resource in the library.

3. When you need information on a topic, do a _____ search.

4. When your search is completed, you should always _____the result list by pressing_____.

5. The column labeled_____will tell you if the item is available or not.

6. If your search did not give you the sources you need, consider truncation as one way to _____ the search.

7. Using a key phrase will make your search more _____.

8. Another way to make a search more specific is to combine terms using _____.

9. When you evaluate sources to decide which would be the most useful, consider both the _____ and_____. To determine if a source is relevant to your topic, look at the _____ and _____ headings.

10. If you connect key words using the Boolean_____, it will make the search broader.

11. If you want a printout of useful sources, first_____ any unwanted items and press_____.

12. The Regular Catalog is useful locating _____ or _____, but when looking for information on a topic, use_____searching.

Library Catalog

Name _____ **Teacher/Period** _____ /

1. At the Library Network Main Menu, select <u>Library Catalog</u>. On the top line of the key-word search screen, type **Russia**. Press **Enter**.

   How many materials were found?_____ Sort the list.
   What is the complete call number of the first source on the list? _____

2. Press **Escape** to return to the search screen. Clear the screen by pressing ____.

3. Enter **Russia*.** (Get * by holding the shift key and pressing the number 8 key.) This is called **truncation**. It abbreviates a key word and tells the computer that you want records which contain either the word **Russia** OR _____.

4. How many materials were found? _____ **Sort** the list.

5. Who is the author of the second source on the list?_____
   (**Hint**: If the entire name of an author does not display, look at the complete record.)

6. Look at the records for **641.5 Lap** and **641.5 Pap**. What are these books about?

   Would either of them be useful? Explain your answer.

7. **Page down**. Look at records for **914.7 Sal** and **947 Rus**. Which of these sources do you think would be the most useful? Explain your answer.

8. How many "hits" do you get with **soviet union**? (no caps needed) _____

9. Try these searches and record the number of "hits" you get.

commonwealth	_____
commonwealth AND states	_____
baltic AND states	_____
central AND asia*	_____
former AND soviet	_____

10. Using the Boolean _____ makes the search more specific. Sometimes this is good. Materials will be more relevant to your topic, but you may overlook some useful general materials. When searching <u>Library Catalog</u>, it is usually best to be more general.

11. Return to the search screen. Enter **Russia**. Arrow down to the next line. Press F2. This changes the _____ from AND to _____ . Add Soviet Union.

12. Did you get more or fewer "hits" this way? _____ Using OR makes the

    search more _____ .

13. Pretend that you have to do a report on one of the following independent states. **Siberia, Tajikistan, Uzbekistan, Azerbaijan, Estonia, Kyrgyzstan, Ukraine, Moldova, Kazakhstan, Belarus, Latvia, Lithuania, or Turkmenistan.**

    Select a topic. Circle your choice. Do a search of this topic.
    Decide which source you think would be the most useful. Fill in the following:
    Title: _____

    Author: _____

    Complete call number: _____

    Copyright date: _____

    Number or pages: _____

14. **Escape** and **clear**. Exit from the Library Catalog until you are back at the Main Menu. Now the work station is ready for the next user.

21 MAGAZINE ARTICLE SUMMARIES

(Note: *Magazine Article Summaries* [*MAS*] from Ebsco is an indexing tool used in many libraries. If you use a different tool, you will need to revise portions of this lesson relating to specific search commands and options. However, the basic search concepts remain the same.)

AUDIENCE

Eighth-grade life science students researching infectious diseases. It is expected that students have already defined the information need. They have located information in general and specialized references and used the library catalog to locate sources in the general collection.

INSTRUCTIONAL OBJECTIVES

1. The learner will gain an understanding of *MAS* as a location tool.
2. The learner will search *MAS* to explore the effects of
   - key-word and key-phrase searching
   - Boolean connectors
   - truncation
   - narrowing and broadening a search with related terms.
3. The learner will evaluate the results of a search to determine their usefulness.
4. The learner will locate, read, and summarize one magazine article on a specified topic.

INFORMATION LITERACY OBJECTIVES

Locate Information

Locate sources
Find information within sources
Scan, screen, and select appropriate resources

Process Information

Interpret the information within a source
Extract information from a source

ANTICIPATORY SET

So far we have defined the information need and developed a research plan to locate information. You have extracted information from reference sources. You have had an opportunity to use one of the library network work stations. What tool did you use? *(Library Catalog)* What sources can you locate using Library Catalog? *(print and nonprint sources in the general collection)*

At the Library Network Main Menu, to use Library Catalog, you selected tool #1. *Did anyone notice the next tool on that menu? What was it? (MAS)* What is it used for? *(to locate magazine articles on various topics by doing key word searches)* Give a general description of *MAS* including the number and type of magazines indexed, the chronological scope of indexing, etc. Today you are going to learn about another tool that can help you locate sources of information.

OBJECTIVE AND PURPOSE STATEMENT

The purpose of today's lesson is to show you how to use *Magazine Article Summaries,* or *MAS,* to locate magazine articles. You will review the electronic search strategies you learned with Library Catalog and learn a few new ones, too.

INSTRUCTIONAL INPUT / MODELING / CHECK FOR UNDERSTANDING

The following is a script for instructional input, including a demonstration with accompanying note-taking guide and question and answer checks for understanding. Modeling is to be done using large screen display to project the *MAS* screen from the computer. It is intended as a sample demonstration that includes the basic operation of *MAS* as well as key concepts related to electronic searching and should be adapted to fit the curriculum and resources of each media center. (Distribute note-taking form.)

MAS Demo Script

1. At the Library Network Main Menu, select *Magazine Article Summaries.* Press 2; Enter. This displays the *MAS* search screen. Here you can do many of the same things you were able to do with Library Catalog—search using key words or phrases, use Boolean connectors to combine key words, truncate, narrow or broaden searches using related terms, print results.
2. Let's say that you are interested in locating magazine articles on the topic of basketball. On the top line of the search screen, enter basketball. Point out that the search was halted at 1,000. This is because the search was too general or broad. We could narrow the search by looking for a specific level of the sport, such as college or professional. We could narrow to a specific team or player.
3. Press Escape. This time let's try basketball ALONG WITH Magic. Explain that ALONG WITH in *MAS* has the same effect as AND in the Library Catalog. Do you think we will get

more hits or fewer? Why? (*fewer, because ALONG WITH narrows the search. The record will have to contain both of these key words.*)

4. *How many hits did we get?* The search yields a list of citations that appear in chronological order starting with the most recent articles and going back to 1984. Mention available indexing for articles prior to 1984. Point out the parts of the citation (subject, title of the article, author, source—name of the magazine, date, page, length, additional information, such as illustrations, maps, and so forth).

5. Ask students to answer questions such as, What is the title of the article in citation 3? How long is the article in citation 2? In what magazine does the article in citation 4 appear? On what page does the article in citation 5 begin? When was article 2 published? Are there any visual aids included with article 4? What does article 3 appear to be about?

6. Sometimes it is possible to tell what the article will be about from the subject heading or the title. Sometimes it is difficult and you need more information before you can decide if an article is relevant to your topic. Show a summary. Mention that this is sometimes called an abstract. If you take the time to read the summary or abstract, there is a better chance that the article will be useful.

7. Not all records will display on one screen. You could hit down arrow key, but it is easier to use Page Down. Pg Dn to other citations. Look at several summaries. Point out that some articles are about Magic Johnson and others are about the team Orlando Magic. Let's try another search.

8. Try basketball ALONG WITH Magic BUT NOT orlando. (Caps not needed.) Do you think we will get more hits or fewer? Why? (*fewer, because BUT NOT will narrow the search by excluding some articles*)

9. How many hits did we get? Did we eliminate the articles dealing with the Orlando Magic? Try basketball ALONG WITH Magic BUT NOT johnson.

10. HINT: In Library Catalog, we learned that it was usually best to be more general; then narrow, if needed. In *MAS,* if you are too general, you will end up with too much information or information that is not relevant. In *MAS,* it is better to start more specific, and then broaden, if necessary.

11. One way to narrow a search is to combine terms using the Boolean ALONG WITH. Another way to narrow is to use the Boolean BUT NOT. Another way you can be more specific is to use a key phrase. Clear the search screen with F9. Let's try orlando magic. Review parts of citations and evaluate relevance.

12. Return to search screen. Clear with F9. Try magic johnson. Try magic ALONG WITH johnson. Compare results. Caution students against inverted names.

13. Let's say that you want articles about Magic Johnson, but you are more interested in his basketball career or family life, not in his ordeal with HIV or AIDS. Try Magic ALONG WITH Johnson BUT NOT HIV OR AIDS. Will this narrow or broaden the search? Why? (*narrow, because it will exclude all the articles about Magic that emphasize HIV or AIDS*)

14. Explain how to use the Boolean OR and how this procedure is different in *MAS* from Library Catalog.

15. Let's say that you are interested in the topic of steroids, especially as they pertain to the world of sports. What search statement should we use? Brainstorm possibilities and the effects of various combinations of key words and Booleans.

16. Try steroids. How many hits did we get? Will they all be relevant? Why not? (*no, because they do not necessarily relate to sports*) Try steroids ALONG WITH sports. How many hits did we get?

17. Now try steroids ALONG WITH athletes. How many hits did we get?

18. You are interested in finding articles that deal with steroids and an athlete, athletes, athletic participation, or athletics. With Library Catalog, you learned a trick to look for different forms of a word. What is that method called? (*truncation*) How do you truncate a key word? (*with an asterisk*)

19. Try steroid* ALONG WITH athlet*. Did we get more hits by truncating? Look at several citations to note the effect of truncation. Point out length of article, including those less than a page. Point out the citations that are highlighted, indicating that they are in the collection. Show the local notes and explain the inter-library loan possibilities or availability at a public library.

20. So far we have tried search strategies we learned with Library Catalog, such as key words, key phrases, Boolean connectors of ALONG WITH, OR, and BUT NOT, truncation, and related terms. *MAS* has some additional search features that Library Catalog does not have. Now we will learn about some of those.

21. As we looked at citations, we noticed that some of the articles are very short—less than one page. An article that short may not be as useful as a longer, more in-depth article. It is possible with *MAS* to specify that you want articles of a certain length. Return to the previous search steroid* ALONG WITH athlet*. Arrow down to the prompt for number of pages. If we enter >1, our search will result in citations about steroid use among athletes, but the articles will be one page or longer. Execute the search and scan citations. Delete >1.

22. Although *MAS* indexes articles back to 1984, you may not want information that old. If you need more current articles, it is possible to specify a date range in your search statement. Arrow down to prompt for date range. Demonstrate how to limit by date. Execute search and scan citations. Delete dates.

23. If you need an article that includes illustrations, it is possible to limit the search to such articles. Demonstrate this search feature. Execute the search and scan citations. Delete this limiter.

24. Cover articles tend to be longer, more in-depth. If you want to see if there are any cover articles on your topic, it is possible to limit your search in this way. Demonstrate this search feature. Execute search; scan citations. Delete limiter.

25. Let's try a new search. Clear search screen with F9. Let's say you are interested in information about Lyle Alzado, a football player who used steroids. Search lyle ALONG WITH alzado. How many hits did we get?

26. Let's say you remember that *Sports Illustrated* did a big article a few years ago on Alzado and the illness he developed from steroid use. Sometimes it is useful to look for articles in a specific magazine. Limit search to *Sports Illustrated*. Do you think we will get more hits or fewer? Why? (*fewer, because the search will exclude articles that are not in this magazine*) Demonstrate this search feature. Execute search; scan citations. Leave this limiter.

27. Now you also remember that Alzado was on the cover. Limit to cover stories. Execute this search. This results in one hit. Scan summary to see if all limiters have been met.

28. Return to search screen and clear. Execute search of steroids. Scan local notes. Remind students that not all of the articles in the result list are holdings in your media center. Emphasize other options for access, such as fax. If, however, you need an article now and cannot wait for a fax or to get to another library, it is possible to limit the search to only magazines in that library. Point out the F4 limiter feature. At the Limit search to library holdings prompt, enter Y. Do you think we will get more hits or fewer? Why? (*fewer, because the search will exclude articles that are not in this library*) Demonstrate this feature. Execute the search.

29. It is possible to get a printout listing the articles you want. Before you do this, it is important to read the summaries to make certain that the articles are useful. Scan several summaries to evaluate the relevance, length or scope, currency, availability, etc. Remind students that these are the same criteria for evaluating sources that were discussed in previous lessons.

30. If you determine that an article would be useful, select it for

inclusion on the printout by pressing F2. This highlights the citation. Review the difference between deletion of titles in Library Catalog and selection in *MAS*. When the selection process is complete, press F6 to print. Point out the choices of citation or abstract and review the difference. Explain the printing process, magazine check-out process, or any special rules which exist in your media center.

GUIDED PRACTICE

Students will work in small groups to complete the activity. The media specialist and teacher will check progress as they practice searches.

INDEPENDENT PRACTICE

Each student will locate one magazine article on a specific disease. The student will read and summarize its contents and cite it appropriately in a bibliography.

To access the activity sheet for the *Magazine Article Summaries* lesson on CD-ROM:

1. Open the CD-ROM and go to the Chapter 21 Folder.
2. Click to open the Folder.
3. Scroll to the *MAS* Activity Sheet.
4. Click to open.

There is also a note-taking guide to help students record and remember lesson input for this lesson on the CD-ROM. To use the note-taking guide:

1. Open the CD-ROM and go to the Chapter 21 Folder.
2. Click to open the Folder.
3. Scroll down to the Note-Taking Guide File.
4. Click to open.

Magazine Article Summaries Note-Taking Guide

1. *MAS* is a_____ to help you locate information in_____.

2. You can search by key word and use the_____connector ALONG WITH to_____a search.

3. In *MAS,* a search results in a list of_____.

4. An important part of the citation is the_____because it tells where the article is located, how current it is, and how long it is.

5. To determine if an article is relevant, read the _____.

6. The Boolean BUT NOT_____a search.

7. In Library Catalog, it is best to begin a search with_____terms. In *MAS,* be more_____.

8. In *MAS,* key words can be entered on the same line and connected with the Boolean_____.

9. Searching various forms of a key word is called_____. This is a way to_____a search.

10. To determine the availability of an article, read the_____ .

11. Searches can be limited by:

    • _____
    • _____
    • _____
    • _____
    • _____
    • _____

12. To get a printout, use F2 to _____ articles.   Then press F6 and choose either the _____ or_____.

Magazine Article Summaries

Name _____   Teacher/Period _____ / ____

1. At the Library Network Main Menu, select *Magazine Article Summaries.* On the top line of the search screen, type disease. Press **F2** to execute the search.

   How many "hits" did you get? _____ What does this tell you? _____

   _____

2. Try **disease** ALONG WITH **infectious**. How many "hits" did you get? _____

3. Try **disease** ALONG WITH **infect***. Truncating will search for various forms of

   the word such as infect, infected, infectious, or infection. How many "hits" did

   you get? _____ Truncation is a way to _____ a search.

4. Is this a good search strategy if your topic is Lyme disease?   Explain.

5. Clear the screen with **F9**. Try lyme. How many "hits" did you get? _____

   Try **lyme** ALONG WITH **disease**. How many "hits" did you get? _____

   Try **lyme disease**. How many "hits" did you get?   _____

   The Boolean ALONG WITH or a key phrase will _____ a search.

6. Look at the first citation. What is the subject heading for this article? _____

   _____

7. Read the summary for this article. Answer the following:

   What is the title of the article? _____

   In what magazine does it appear? _____

   What is the date of the article? _____

   How long is it? _____

   In what libraries is this available? _____

   Do you think this article would be useful? _____ Explain your answer.

8. Try **hepatitis**. How many "hits" did you get? _____

9.   Try **ecoli**. How many "hits" did you get? _____ Why do you think this

     happened? _____

     Now try **e coli**. What happens? _____

10. Try **e coli or escherichia coli** all on the same line. How many "hits" did you

     get? _____ Using the Boolean OR will _____ a search.

11. Try **infectious** OR **communicable** (all on the same line) ALONG WITH

     disease. Look back at question #2. How are these two searches different?

     _____

12. Sometimes looking at the subject headings in the citation can give you ideas for

     other key words to try. Execute a search of **ebola**. List two subject headings

     that appear frequently. _____

     _____

13. Try the phrase **Rocky Mountain Spotted Fever**. List two subject headings

     that appear frequently. _____

     _____

14. Search **cold** (as in the disease). How many "hits" did you get? _____

     Explain whether this is a good strategy.

15. Try **cold** BUT NOT **war**. What effect does the Boolean BUT NOT have?

16. Search **herpes**. Limit your search to articles that are >1 page and are in this

     library. Scan the summaries and select **one** article you feel would be useful.

     Print the abstract for this article. **Attach the printout to this sheet**!

17. Execute a search of your own topic for this class. Locate one article to use for

     your research. Check the magazine out, photocopy the article, or request a fax

     if you need to get it from another library.

18. Read the article. Summarize what you learned. Remember to cite this source

     on your bibliography!

22 FUNDAMENTAL CONCEPTS OF ELECTRONIC INFORMATION ACCESS TOOLS

AUDIENCE

All ninth-grade students as part of the basic information literacy lessons taught in English classes or some other core curricular area. This lesson assumes that students have already learned and had some experience using several different electronic information access tools.

INSTRUCTIONAL OBJECTIVE

The learner will use the search/find features commonly found in electronic information access tools (e.g., Library Catalog, *MAS*, *NewsBank*, *SIRS*, WWW).

INFORMATION LITERACY OBJECTIVES

Locate Information

Locate sources

ANTICIPATORY SET

(Distribute Note-Taking Guide.) For every source of information, there is a tool to provide assistance in finding the information efficiently. Name the tools that correspond to various sources of information. (Use transparency on page 226.)

Tools	Finding Aid
World Book Encyclopedia	index volume
Encarta	search screen
our library's books and videos	Library Catalog
public library books and videos	college or university library
magazine articles	*MAS* or *Readers' Guide* or InfoTrac
newspaper articles	*NewsBank*
World Wide Web (WWW)	Alta Vista

OBJECTIVE AND PURPOSE STATEMENT

Many of the information access tools being developed today are electronic, making use of computer technology to allow us to locate sources of information efficiently. As you have discovered by now, these electronic tools all operate somewhat differently. The search screens give you different options, function keys are not standardized, and the way one sorts, selects, and prints out results varies from tool to tool. Despite the differences, every electronic search tool is based on a few fundamental concepts. If you are familiar with these concepts, you should be able to adapt to and operate any electronic information access tool you encounter.

INSTRUCTIONAL INPUT / MODELING / CHECK FOR UNDERSTANDING

1. Electronic information access tools allow searching on the basis of key words. Key words (or key phrases) are those words that relate to the topic being researched. Consider various forms of the words, alternate spellings, and related words (more specific and more general). Be prepared to use different key words in the different tools. For example, it is usually more productive to use more general key words in a library catalog and more specific key words in a periodical index. Be persistent. Try a number of key-word searches to find the most productive for a particular tool.

   • The topic is American sports during World War II. Brainstorm key words. Record ideas on the transparency on page 229. (*sports, athletics, leisure, baseball, football, professional, WW II, World War II, WW2, World War Two*)

2. Truncation is a technique used in most electronic tools. By entering just the root of a key word followed by some sort of truncation character, all forms of that word will be searched and identified. Truncation is particularly helpful in finding plural forms of words. Most of our tools currently use the * as the truncation character, but occasionally the ? is used. Someday, electronic tools will be intuitive enough to automatically do the truncation for us (in fact, some already do plurals), but until then, it is up to us!

   • Would it be useful to truncate any of the key words in the American sports during WW II search? (*athletics*) How should we truncate? Record ideas on a transparency. (*athletic* = athletic, athletics, athletically; athlet* = athletic, athletics, athletically, athlete, athletes*)

3. Boolean connectors allow the linking of key words in various ways to refine searches. What are the three Boolean connectors?

(AND, OR, NOT) Which connector should be used to narrow a search? *(AND)* Which connector broadens a search when linking key words? *(OR)* The NOT connector is not used very often, but what effect does its use have on a search? *(narrows, fewer hits)* There are some limitations with most of our electronic tools today, in that only a certain number of key words can be used in any one search. (e.g. Library Catalog allows only three, *MAS* allows four.) Some are restrictive in how the connectors are placed; others (for example, *NewsBank)* allow search statements to be written out like a math statement, using parentheses to indicate how the key words are to be grouped.

- Construct a search statement (key words + Boolean connectors) that will find bibliographic records dealing with American sports during WW II. Record ideas on the transparency. *([sports or athlet*] and World War II)*
- How could this search be narrowed? *(add "AND America"; add "NOT baseball")*
- How could this search be broadened? *([sports or athlet*] and [World War II or WW II])*

4. After executing a search of any electronic tool, it is important to do a quick assessment to determine whether the results are reasonable or not.

- If a *MAS* search on "athletes" yields zero hits, this is not reasonable. What are some plausible reasons for zero results? Record ideas on the transparency. *(incorrect spelling, key word entered on the wrong line on the screen)*
- If a Library Catalog search on "WW II" yields only eight hits, this is not reasonable. How should the search be adjusted? *(try WWII or World War II or World War Two)*
- If a *NewsBank* search on "sports and World War II" yields one hit, this might be reasonable. (Consider that *NewsBank* covers newspaper articles from 1994 to the present. It probably is not the most appropriate source to use for this topic!)

Often searches need to be adjusted and re-executed to discover and put together the most productive key words. Don't be afraid to try different searches. While some key words may work well with a particular tool, another tool may require different key words to be productive.

5. Try some searches in a few of our tools. The topic is music labeling—whether music should be labeled or rated the way films are. (Use data/video display panel to demonstrate in Library Catalog. Ask students to suggest possible search statements. Try

to show the following points, asking what is being searched with each.)

music labeling	0 hits	(phrase, terms must be in this order)
labeling of music	0 hits	(phrase, terms must be in this order)
music AND labeling	0 hits	(separate key words, better than above)
music AND label*	1 hit	(Truncation is the difference. See page 222.)
music AND censor*	4 hits	(See Chapter 5 as well as page 222—ideas of related key words.)
freedom of speech	10 hits	(much more general, may have a chapter . . .)

Try searches in *MAS* on the same topic.

- What are some general observations comparing Library Catalog and *MAS*? *MAS* is a much larger database, with lengthier annotations, so key-word searches generally yield many more hits.
- Use more general key words in Library Catalog, more specific key words in *MAS*. When using a full-text tool like *NewsBank* or *SIRS* or WebCrawler, this is even more evident.

GUIDED PRACTICE

Students work in groups to complete the activity below, presenting their findings to the entire class.

INDEPENDENT PRACTICE

To be determined by the teacher or library media specialist based on curricular unit.

To use the transparencies for this lesson on CD-ROM:

1. Open the CD-ROM and go to the Chapter 22 Folder.
2. Click to open the Folder.
3. Scroll down to Fundamental Concepts: Electronic Tools 1 and 2
4. Click to open.

There is also a note-taking guide and activity for this lesson on the CD-ROM. To use the note-taking guide:

1. Open the CD-ROM and go to the Chapter 22 Folder.
2. Click to open the Folder.
3. Scroll down to the desired file.
4. Click to open.

Fundamental Concepts of Electronic Information Access Tools

Note-Taking Guide

1. To locate sources of information, use various

2. Most electronic tools are based on four fundamental concepts:

    • _____   • _____

    • _____   • _____

3. When identifying key words, consider

    • _____   • _____

    • _____   • _____

4. Two common truncation characters are _____ and _____ .

5. When key words are linked with the Boolean connector **AND**, the result list is _____ .

6. When key words are linked with the Boolean connector **OR**, the result list is _____ .

7. If a search results in too few hits, the search may be broadened in several ways:

    • _____

    • _____

    • _____

8. If a search results in too many hits, the search may be narrowed in several ways:

    • _____

    • _____

    • _____

Fundamental Concepts – Electronic Tools

World Book Encyclopedia

Encarta

books and videos in the school library

books and videos in the public library

magazine articles

newspaper articles

Internet (WWW)

Fundamental Concepts–Electronic Tools

key word

truncation

Boolean connectors

assessment

Fundamental Concepts–Electronic Tools #1

With the other students in your group, consider one of the research topics marked
below: (Media specialist preassigns topics.)

violence on television	**animal rights**
date rape	**interracial adoption**
police brutality	**organ transplantation**
affirmative action	**sexual harassment**

1. Brainstorm possible **key words**. Record all ideas on the transparency.

2. Consider which key words could be **truncated**. Record on the transparency.

3. Consider how keywords could be linked with **Boolean connectors**. Record
    ideas on the transparency.

4. At a Library Network workstation execute a search in *Magazine Article
    Summaries* to find magazine articles on the topic. You may need to try several
    searches to get the right combination of key words and Boolean connectors. On
    the transparency, record the search as you executed it.

*Be prepared to present your findings to the entire class. Show and explain the
transparency you have made on the form provided. On the demonstration workstation,
show the search/searches you executed and explain which search was the most
effective.*

Fundamental Concepts–Electronic Tools #2

Topic

Keywords

Truncation

Boolean

Searches executed in *MAS*

23 FOCUSING A RESEARCH TOPIC

AUDIENCE

Ninth- and tenth-grade English classes preparing for research projects. This lesson can be adapted for other grade levels and curricular areas.

INSTRUCTIONAL OBJECTIVES

1. The learner will practice three methods for narrowing a research topic.
2. The learner will locate one source for background information on a topic.
3. The learner will read and summarize the information on the selected topic.

INFORMATION LITERACY OBJECTIVES

Define the Information Need

Decide what information is needed

Locate Information

Develop a research plan
Find information within a source

Process Information

Extract information from a source

ANTICIPATORY SET

During the next few weeks you will each be undertaking a significant project: researching and writing a paper on a topic of interest. Your English teacher has already introduced this project to you and given you a thick packet that describes in detail the various steps involved in this project. This guide will be very useful to you in the days ahead.

I hope that you have been thinking about your topics. Choosing a topic is one of the critical moments in a research project. It must be a subject you are interested in. It is generally helpful if you know something about the topic. This will help you get started. Also, if you select a topic that interests you, the desire to learn more will motivate you as you conduct your research.

The second consideration is to select a topic that is manageable: not too general, not too specific, and one for which information is readily available to you. If the topic is too narrow, it may be difficult to find information, leading to frustration. If the topic is too broad, there may be too much information, making your task overwhelming.

Today we are going to do two activities to get you on the right track for your upcoming research. First, we are going to discuss and practice giving focus to topics. In my experience, the number one problem students encounter has to do with topic selection. Using the library is generally not a problem: most students can locate information—or they ask for assistance. Taking notes is generally not a problem: most students can handle this. Writing the bibliography is not difficult, as long as you keep track of your sources as you use them and record the sources in the correct format, using the examples in your packet. But it all goes back to having a focused topic. If your topic is not clearly defined and refined, you will face roadblocks along the way. If you carefully choose your topic, your efforts will go more smoothly and be less stressful!

We will cover how to focus a topic. Then, I will give you each a chance to do some general reading and summary writing about your topic.

During this period, you will learn three techniques for narrowing a topic. You will practice these techniques to focus your own research topic. You will then locate one source in our library that provides some general information about your topic. You will read this background information and summarize your findings. By the end of the period, each of you should have a grasp of where you will be heading with your research during the next days.

INSTRUCTIONAL INPUT (The following is a script for instructional activity.)

Your teacher distributed to you a list of suggested topics. These are very broad topics—much too general to be useful as they stand—but any of these could be molded into an appropriate research topic. For example, sports is on the list. This is too broad. I could narrow this topic to baseball. This is still too broad, so I need to further refine my focus. Depending on my interest, I could research the history of baseball uniforms or how one becomes an umpire. I could research the old Negro Leagues or the racial integration of baseball. There has been a lot in the media about discrimination in baseball. I'd like to answer the questions, "How are minorities treated in baseball? How have conditions changed since the days of Jackie Robinson?"

Or I could go in a different direction: Are there are any female umpires? Cincinnati has had a female owner. How many female owners have there been? How did they become owners? What problems are encountered between a female owner and the male players?

Clearly, a research topic is like Playdough. You can change its size and shape to fit your own design. I just demonstrated several techniques for narrowing a topic. Now we are going to practice three of these techniques together.

MODELING

1. Narrowing a general subject by naming subtopics. Start with a general idea and explore possible subtopics. Perhaps one item on the list can become the basis of your research paper. For example, See transparency on Narrowing with Subtopics. If students have difficulty thinking of subtopics, suggest these:

   Education: violence in schools, drugs in schools, graduation requirements, a college of interest (history, admissions, course offerings, cost, etc.), how the U.S. compares to other nations academically, the role of sports in schools, Head Start, foreign language instruction, vocational classes, school bond issues, gender bias in education, etc.

   Business: mandatory retirement age, minorities in business, migrant workers, farming as a business, the flight of U.S. business to foreign countries, the impact of NAFTA, investments, opening your own business, "hot" business prospects for future employment, etc.

   Medical ethics: euthanasia (Discuss use of synonymous terms such as mercy killing or doctor-assisted suicide), cloning, animal experimentation, psychiatric commitments, brain death, living wills, or advanced directives.

2. Narrowing a general subject by clustering. Some researchers begin with a general idea and cluster ideas around it. Sometimes this technique is known as creating "a web." For example, See transparency on Narrowing by Clustering. If students have difficulty, suggest possible connections such as TV commercials aimed at children, a parent's right to limit a child's TV viewing, TV electronics as a health risk, the ethics of electronically recording TV programming or intercepting cable without paying, why children can handle the electronics of TV (VCRs) better than parents, electronic games played via TV, and so forth.

3. Narrowing a general subject by asking questions. A research question can serve two important functions. It can address a specific issue or problem that you may wish to investigate. It can also provoke an answer and thereby produce a possible thesis statement. In either case you will bring a needed focus to your entire paper. For example, See transparency on Narrowing with Questions. If needed, suggest:

Censorship: Are movie ratings a form of censorship? What censorship laws exist in our state? Should pornography be censored? Should cigarette manufacturers be allowed to sponsor sporting events on TV? What are frequently censored books?

Desert Storm: What events led to Desert Storm? Should the U.S. have become involved? What was the role of women or should women be in combat? What contribution was made by other nations? (This could be done with other areas of foreign policy such as Bosnia or Somalia.)

Bilingualism: Should English be declared our national language? Should schools be expected to meet the needs of all bilingual students? What problems do residents of Quebec face?

INDEPENDENT PRACTICE

After modeling each technique, the students will be given several minutes to practice the technique to narrow their own topics. This exercise will be done on the Activity sheet labeled Focusing a Research Topic. The media specialist and teacher will circulate to check for understanding and assist as needed.

After focusing their topics, students will be directed to locate some general background information on the topic by completing the following activity.

To use the transparencies and activity sheet for this lesson on CD-ROM:

1. Open the CD-ROM and go to the Chapter 23 Folder.
2. Click to open the Folder.
3. Scroll to the needed files.
4. Click to open.

Focusing a Research Topic

Narrowing a general subject with subtopics

education	**year-long school calendar**
	technology in school
	_____
	_____

business	**minimum wage**
	age discrimination
	sexual harassment
	_____
	_____

medical ethics	**euthanasia**
	organ transplantation
	_____
	_____
	_____
	_____

Focusing a Research Topic

Narrowing a subject by clustering

children

electronics

television

parents

Focusing a Research Topic

Narrowing a subject by asking questions

censorship

_____

_____

_____

Desert Storm

_____

_____

_____

bilingualism

_____

_____

_____

Focusing a Research Topic

Name _____ **Teacher/Period** _____ / _____

Topic _____

1. List **subtopics** that relate to your general topic.

   _____

   _____

   _____

2. Create a web by **clustering** ideas around your general topic.

3. Ask **questions** suggested by your general topic.

   _____

   _____

   _____

   _____

4. Locate one source in our library which provides some general information about your topic. (A general or specialized encyclopedia is a good place to begin with this background reading.) Read the article or introductory chapter and write below a summary of what you learned about your topic.

_____

_____

_____

_____

_____

_____

_____

_____

_____

_____

_____

_____

_____

Source: (Record here the relevant bibliographic information for the source used.)

_____

_____

5. Did your preliminary reading suggest any subtopics or questions which you could use as the basis of your research paper? If so, what?

_____

_____

_____

_____

_____

24 NEWSBANK

(Note: While this lesson is designed for use with *NewsBank*, it could be adapted to other full-text news article sources.)

AUDIENCE
Ninth-grade language arts classes.

INSTRUCTIONAL OBJECTIVE
The learner will use the various features of *NewsBank* to locate and access articles.

INFORMATION LITERACY OBJECTIVE

Locate Information
Find information within sources
Scan, screen, and select suitable sources

Process Information
Interpret the information within a source
Evaluate the usefulness of the information
Extract information from a source

ANTICIPATORY SET
(Distribute note-taking guide)
Show a newspaper article and show the various parts. Discuss how

- headlines that are often created to catch attention do not provide key words for searching.
- key words can have two meanings.

(Transparency : Make a transparency of a newspaper article)
The purpose of this lesson is to acquaint you with the capabilities of the *NewsBank* full-text retrieval system. It should provide you with the basics that would allow you to use other full-text information sources.

INSTRUCTIONAL INPUT
NewsBank is a CD that is located on the server and can be accessed through Library Network stations. It contains full-text articles of current issues and events selected from over 100 newspapers from across Canada and the United States. Additional articles are selected from American and International news wires that provide current up-to-date information.

1. *NewsBank* is full text which means it is both a tool and a source.

   - First, we will concentrate on searching *NewsBank*; using it as a tool to search for useful information.
   - Then we will discuss how to engage the information within the source.

   (Use a large screen display from the computer to provide visual clarification and reinforcement of the following points.)

2. You must select which database you wish to access. You can either select the *NewsBank* Core or Spanish Language. Your search statement must be in Spanish to search the Spanish Language database.

3. Next select the year you want to search, 1994 or 1995.

4. *NewsBank* provides for two levels of searching.

   - Level I = conduct a broad key-word search. It is not possible at this level to refine your search as well.
   - Level II = customize the search according to which fields will be most relevant to your search.

   For most of your searching needs, Level II would be a better choice.

5. The available fields in Level II enable you to create a search statement that will access those articles that will provide the most useful information. The fields include

All Text	Same as Level I; locates key words anywhere in the article.
Headlines	Can be misleading; headlines often are simply to catch attention or to be cute by using a play on words.
Lead	From the lead paragraph of the article. If it is good journalism, the key words should be located in the lead paragraph, so this is better than just headlines.
Index Terms	Key words that have been assigned to the article by *NewsBank* readers. It is sometimes advisable to search by key word in All Text and when you find an article that fits your needs, check the Index Terms.
Author	If you are searching for a specific author.

Date	Limits the search to a certain date or range of dates. Use the following formula. *Note: no commas.* February 26 1995 to March 31 1995 *or* >April 15 1995 (articles *after* date; use < for articles *before*).
Source	Limits the search to articles originating from a particular newspaper or wire service. The best way to check spelling of the name of a newspaper is to highlight the Source field and press F5. (Use *Des Moines Register* or another newspaper in the database as an example.)

6. Now that the search has been completed, we need to switch from using *NewsBank* as a searching tool to using it as a source of information. The function keys are used to move from the tool to the source.

   - *F7* displays the headlines of the articles from your search statement.
   - *F8* displays full text from the highlighted headline.
   - *F3* marks (and unmarks) an article for printing.
   - *F4* prints selected articles.
   - *F1* returns to the search screen to start a new search; returns to the tool.

7. Viewing the full text of article:

   - Press the down arrow or the PageDown key to view more of the current article.
   - Press the up arrow or PageUp key to review text in the current article.
   - Press the right arrow key to view the next article.
   - Press the left arrow key to view the previous article.

Each occurrence of your search term(s) in the text of an article is called a hit. To jump to the next hit press the Tab key.

8. *NewsBank* allows you to select part of the article for printing. This is a great way to cut down on the amount of paper you have to deal with. To mark lines of text for printing

   - Move the cursor to the first line you wish to mark.
   - Hold down the Shift key.
   - Press the Down arrow key until all the text you wish to mark is highlighted.

You can repeat this process to mark other lines or paragraphs anywhere else in the current article and in other articles.

9. Your printing options are

- Article with Citation includes the full text of the article plus bibliographic information.
- Citation Only includes bibliographic information only.
- Print Screen includes all the information currently displayed on your screen.

10. You can print the Current Article, Marked Article, or All Articles. If you selected Marked Article and you have marked partial articles the bibliographic information will automatically be added to your printout.

GUIDED PRACTICE

Students work in small groups of four or fewer depending upon the size of the class to complete the activity sheets that follow. Each group will then exchange sheets with the group who did the other activity and check the search statement, strategy, and results of the other group. Evaluation will include both their own search statements and their suggestions pertaining to the other group's search statements.

INDEPENDENT PRACTICE

To be determined by the teacher and the library media specialist based upon a curricular unit.

To access the activity sheets for the *NewsBank* lesson on CD-ROM:

1. Open the CD-ROM and go to the Chapter 24 Folder.
2. Click to open the Folder.
3. Scroll to the *NewsBank* Activity or *NewsBank* Advanced Search Activity.
4. Click to open.

Follow the procedure above to access the transparency for this lesson.

There is also a note-taking guide to help students record and remember lesson input for each of these lessons on the CD-ROM. To use the note-taking guides,

1. Open the CD-ROM and go to the Chapter 24 Folder.
2. Click to open the Folder.
3. Scroll down to the Note-taking Guides File.
4. Click to open.

NewsBank Note-Taking Guide

1. *NewsBank* is located on the _____ .

2. *NewsBank* is both a _____ to locate information and a

   _____ of information.

   This is because *NewsBank* is _____ .

3. The two databases you can search in *NewsBank* are_____ and

   _____ .

4. *NewsBank* provides two levels of searching.

   • Level I is used for _____

   • Level II is used for_____

5. In Level II searching, what part of the article will the program look for the search

   statement?

   • All text _____

   • Lead _____

   • Index Terms _____

6. Once your search is completed, use the function keys to display your results.

   _____ displays the headlines of your hits

   _____ displays the full text of the highlighted headline

   _____ marks article for printing

   _____ prints selected articles

7. Often you only need part of the article. To mark the section of the article you want

   printed you

   1. _____

   2. _____

   3. _____

8. The citation is the _____ .

   If you mark only part of the article for printing, will *NewsBank* still print the

   citation?_____

NewsBank

Name _____**Teacher/Period** _____ / _____

Group Members:

_____   _____

_____   _____

> You have been assigned to do research on stalking laws in the United States. You are interested in how state laws differ from state to state and how effective the laws seem to be. Search the NewsBank Core at Level II.

Write your search statement indicating which fields you searched, the statement, and what the results were (# of hits). (Hint: Don't forget Boolean connectors and truncation.)

FIELD	SEARCH STATEMENT	HITS

- Mark the search statement you think produced the most useful information with an (X).

- Explain **why** the articles found by this statement would provide the most useful information for you. (Hint: You will need to scan the articles and evaluate their usefulness.)

Research Reviewed by

_____   _____

_____   _____

NewsBank

Name _____ **Teacher/Period** _____ / _____

Group Members:

_____   _____

_____   _____

You have been assigned to do research on lifting the embargo against Vietnam. What does this mean for US. trade? How do veterans of the Vietnam War feel about it?. Search the NewsBank Core at Level II.

Write your search statement indicating which fields you searched, the statement, and

what the results were (# of hits). (Hint: Don't forget Boolean connectors and truncation.)

FIELD	SEARCH STATEMENT	HITS

- Mark the search statement you think produced the most useful information with an
  (X).

- Explain **why** the articles found by this statement would provide the most useful
  information for you. (Hint: You will need to scan the articles and evaluate their
  usefulness.)

Research Reviewed by

_____   _____

_____   _____

NEWSBANK ADVANCED SEARCHING STRATEGIES

AUDIENCE

It is assumed that the students will already have had experience using different search tools and designing search statements. It would be helpful if the student had completed the basic *NewsBank* lesson.

INSTRUCTIONAL OBJECTIVE

The learner will review Boolean connectors and truncation and learn how to use proximity connectors to refine search statements.

INFORMATION LITERACY OBJECTIVE

Locate Information

Find information within sources

ANTICIPATORY SET

(Distribute note-taking guide.)

Think of writing a search statement as being a little like writing a mathematical formula. The order and the symbols used can make a big difference in what results you get. How would the history of the world be written if Einstein had written $E=cm^2$? The more exacting your assignments get the more you need to refine your search statements so you get the "perfect article" for your research.

OBJECTIVE AND PURPOSE STATEMENT

While Boolean connectors and truncation help in creating a more useful search statement, there are some ways in which the search can be refined. These search statement strategies may vary in different databases and tools, but the principle is the same and will help search at higher levels of effectiveness. Today's lesson will deal specifically with the search strategies employed by *NewsBank*.

INSTRUCTIONAL INPUT

1. Truncation is the technique used to include the variations of a word in the search. Using the root word and adding an asterisk (*) will search for both single and multiple characters. An example is when we use the root word *ecolog** (transparency on page 252). Record student ideas: ecology, ecological, ecologist. . . .

2. *NewsBank* uses "?" to replace a single character. For example, to find articles containing *woman or women,* type *wom?n.*

(For the following use the LCD panel and the *NewsBank* program to model the search statements and show the differences in results.)

3. The Boolean connector AND is used to link two words and will find articles that contain both search terms. For example, if you enter censorship AND music, the articles you find will contain both censorship and music.

Would truncation make a difference in the number and/or type of articles the search found?

4. If you were to use *proximity connectors,* you would refine your search statement even more.

Sames—the articles contain both terms in the same sentence. For example, try using *Clinton Sames Environment* and each article Clinton and environment would appear in the same sentence.

What advantage would this provide that the AND *connector could not? How could this result in a more specific search statement?*

Nearx—the articles contain both terms within x words of each other, in any order. For example, if you enter: Gangs Near2 Violence, the articles you find will contain both gangs and violence, and in each article they will appear within two words of each other in any order.

Adjx—the articles contain both terms within x words of each other in the order entered. For example, if you enter Homeless Adj3 Shelter*, the articles you find will contain both homeless and shelters, and in each article they will appear within three words of each other in the order entered. This search would find "homeless shelters" and "homeless cannot find shelter" but would not find "shelters for the homeless."

5. Structuring the search statement allows you to dictate the order in which the database searches the articles for your terms. As you use AND, NOT, OR to clarify your search statement, you can place parentheses around the terms you want to search first, then search those results with the other term. For example, (Homicide OR Murder) AND Gang? would first locate all the articles dealing with homicide or murder and then look for gang or gangs.

Why did I not want to truncate using the multiple letter symbol*?

(Hint: gangrene.)

Would SAMES *work better than* AND? *Why or why not?*

GUIDED PRACTICE

Students will preplan some search statements that pertain to their research projects, filling out the Search Strategy Worksheet. After having their search strategies reviewed, students will proceed with independent practice. If their search statements do not yield the expected results, students will redo or refine their Search Strategy Worksheet.

INDEPENDENT PRACTICE

To be determined by the teacher and library media specialist based upon a curricular unit.

NewsBank Advanced Searching Strategies
Note-Taking Guide

1. *NewsBank* uses two truncation symbols.

   * is used for _____

   ? is used for _____

2. If you use the Boolean connector AND, articles found in the search will

   contain_____

3. What do the three proximity connectors used in *NewsBank* mean?

   sames _____

   near*x* _____

   adj*x* _____

4. Using parentheses in a search statement will group words together. The

   advantage of this is to _____ .

NewsBank Advanced Searching Strategies

Name _____ **Teacher / Period** _____/_____

Research Topic: _____

_____

Key words or other fitting descriptors you could use in your search statement.

_____   _____

_____   _____

_____   _____

_____   _____

Using Boolean connectors or proximity connectors or parentheses, write at least three

possible search statements.

- _____
- _____
- _____
- _____
- _____

Try your search statements. Look at the results. Mark the statement you think provides

the most useful information for your purposes with an X. Look at the index terms or

other indicators and write at least one new or modified search statement.

- _____
- _____

NewsBank Advanced Searching

Truncating

Ecolog*

What words will the program be searching for if you use this truncated word?

25 FILTERING CRITERIA: EVALUATING SEARCH RESULTS

AUDIENCE
All ninth-grade students as part of the basic information literacy lessons taught in English classes or some other core curricular area. This lesson could be incorporated into a lesson demonstrating the use of a particular tool, including use of the Internet.

INSTRUCTIONAL OBJECTIVE
The learner will evaluate the results of a search by applying filtering criteria to select the most appropriate sources for a particular information need.

INFORMATION LITERACY OBJECTIVES

Locate Information
Scan, screen, and select appropriate resources

ANTICIPATORY SET
You are researching the militia movement—its history in our country, as well as recent developments and actions of some of the more extreme groups.

- What are some possible sources of information on this topic? (*general reference, books, videos, magazines, newspapers, Iowa Militia or National Guard member, WWW*)
- If you want to look for magazine articles, what tool do you use? (Readers' Guide *for pre-1984 articles and* MAS *for articles since 1984*)
- A key-word search of militia in *MAS* results in 200 hits. Will you check out all 200 of these magazines, skim the articles, and select the ones that will be useful to you? (*Not likely! Not necessary!*)

The result of executing a search using an information access tool such as Library Catalog, *MAS*, *Readers' Guide*, *NewsBank*, or *SIRS*, is a list of potentially useful sources of information. Sometimes, this list is quite lengthy. It is inefficient and usually unnecessary for a researcher to look at all of the sources. Rather, by applying some comparative or evaluative criteria to the list of potential sources, it is possible to filter through the list, selecting those sources that will be of greatest value to you. This filtering criteria is the subject of our discussion today.

INSTRUCTIONAL INPUT / CHECK FOR UNDERSTANDING

1. First, it is important to note that you are the one who must decide which of the filtering criteria is relevant and important to consider in any given research situation. For one research problem, currency may be the most important consideration when selecting sources. For another research problem, availability of the source may be the most important consideration. You have to decide.

2. Suitability has to do with whether a particular source will be appropriate and useful for you, based on its level of sophistication. A college-level textbook on genetics may not be as useful as a two-page magazine article on cloning. Be honest in assessing your background knowledge or level of expertise on a particular topic. Select resources that you will be able to understand.

3. Currency is an easier filtering criterion to apply, because it is based on objective data—the publication date of the source. Again, you need to decide whether currency is important for your topic. With some topics you must have recently published sources; with other topics, old sources will work fine.

4. Availability has to do with how easily you can retrieve the source. If a potentially useful book in the collection is currently checked out and you need the information today, you should probably move on to another source. If you discover that there are books on your topic at the public or university libraries, and you don't have time to go downtown or on campus, you should probably try elsewhere. If *MAS* indicates that the school doesn't subscribe to a particular magazine, but it is available from another school in the district, you can ask to have the article faxed to you, often within an hour. If you can wait an hour, fine. If not, try something else. The relative importance of availability as a filtering criterion depends, essentially, on your research timeline.

5. Reliability is much more difficult to judge. First, how credible is the author? With books and magazines, there is usually a little information about the author, and we can assume that if published or produced by a known publisher, there is some cross-checking and editorial control occurring. With other sources, particularly Internet sources, who knows? It is important to continually question the authority of the sources we use—print, electronic, even human. Another aspect related to reliability is point

of view or bias. Does the author/publisher/producer have a bias through which the "information" is being presented? Sometimes this can be ascertained by the bibliographic record; often it is necessary to read or view the information source itself to make the determination.

6. Relevance has to do with whether the information in the source is "on target" for your particular research topic, or if it is unrelated or only marginally related. It is quite common when doing key-word searching in an electronic information access tool to get false hits—references to sources retrieved because the specified key word has a double meaning, one of which is totally unrelated to your topic. These hits are usually easy to filter out. More difficult is handling those references retrieved because the key word was mentioned in passing, perhaps in a summary, a note, or an abstract. Try looking at the subject headings assigned to the source; these might give a clue as to the relevance. Sometimes, looking at the length of an article will give an indication of relative relevance—the scope or depth of the information. Remember: If in doubt (about the relevance), check it out!

7. To help you remember these five filtering criteria, think SCARR. Ask students to name the five filters and describe each briefly.

GUIDED PRACTICE
Students work in groups of four (group size depends on number of available work stations) to complete activity sheets.

INDEPENDENT PRACTICE
To be determined by the teacher or library media specialist based on curricular unit.

To use the transparency for this lesson is located on CD-ROM:

1. Open the CD-ROM and go to the Chapter 25 Folder.
2. Click to open the Folder.
3. Scroll to Evaluating Results File.
4. Click to open.

To access the activity sheet:

1. Open the CD-ROM and go to the Chapter 25 Folder.
2. Click to open the Folder.
3. Scroll to the Filtering Criteria Activity Sheet.
4. Click to open.

Filtering Criteria – Evaluating Search Results

suitability

currency

availability

reliability

relevance

Filtering Criteria: Evaluating Search Results

Name: _____   Teacher/Period: _____ / ___

Name: _____

Name: _____

Name: _____

With the other students in your group, consider the following:

> Since the 1995 bombing of the Federal Building in Oklahoma City, much attention has been given to the "militia movement." While some militia units serve in innocuous, supportive roles, other groups are more extreme in their actions. Survivalists, NeoNazis, Skinheads–these extremist groups are becoming increasingly prevalent in our society.
>
> What are the motivations behind extremist groups? Why do they form? What do they hope to prove or bring about?

1. Execute a search in *MAS* to find magazine articles that would address this issue. What search statement did you use (key words and Boolean connectors)? _____
   _____

   Select and print the abstracts for three articles. Attach the printout to this page.

   On the printout, explain why you chose each of those three articles. (Which filtering criteria did you use and why?)

2. Now, execute a search in *NewsBank* to find newspaper articles which would address this issue. What search statement did you use (keywords and Boolean connectors)? _____

   Select and print the citations (not the full-text!) for two articles. Attach the printout to this page.

   On the printout, explain why you chose each of those two articles. (Which filtering criteria did you use and why?)

Reminder: Stapled behind this page should be two printouts--one from MAS *and one from* NewsBank.

26 LEARNING ACCEPTABLE INTERNET USE

(Note: Our school district has developed an acceptable use agreement for students. That statement is available on our homepage at www.iowa-city.k12.ia.us. Each local school will want to carefully consider whether to adopt such a document and will want to tailor it to local needs. The following lesson is included as an example of how to introduce students to some of the issues they may encounter in using the Internet as an information tool.)

AUDIENCE

All ninth-grade students taking Internet instruction in science classes or some other core curricular area. This lesson should be taught in conjunction with a "how-to" lesson on using the Internet.

INSTRUCTIONAL OBJECTIVE

The learner will understand and demonstrate appropriate, acceptable use of the Internet, as outlined in the school acceptable use agreement.

INFORMATION LITERACY OBJECTIVES

Locate Information

Task: Scan, screen, and select appropriate resources

Process Information

Evaluate information from a source

ANTICIPATORY SET

The Internet is not something new. This complex network of worldwide computer networks has been around for several decades. It's not even that new here at our school. We have been using various portions of the Internet for several years. What is new for us is that we are finally reaching the point where we can easily provide students and teachers access to this resource. More computers and our school district's computer network are making this access easier.

In your science classes, you have been learning your way around the Internet—at least the Web portion of it. Along with learning how to use the Internet, you need to learn about your rights and responsibilities regarding this vast electronic resource. Over the years, we school library media specialists have taught students about different sources of information and the tools that help to locate that information efficiently. The Internet is yet another source of information with several built-in tools. But there is a difference with the Internet. This is not some source or tool that I purchase or subscribe to for the school, and which we can use as we want. Because the Internet is coordinated through an association of agencies and organizations with established guidelines, all end users (any of us!) are responsible for following these policies and procedures. We will discuss what is referred to as "acceptable use" of the Internet.

INSTRUCTIONAL INPUT / MODELING / CHECK FOR UNDERSTANDING

1. Review some Internet basics: Internet, e-mail, Telnet, FTP, gopher, WWW. Briefly demonstrate how to telnet, gopher, and go to the local homepage.
2. The established guidelines for using the Internet include these terms and conditions:

   Acceptable Use. Any use of the Internet at school must be for school-related or research needs. Personal use, commercial activities, or advertisement are not permitted.

   Privileges. The use of the Internet is a privilege, not a right, and inappropriate use will result in cancellation of those privileges.

   Netiquette. All users are expected to abide by the generally accepted rules of network etiquette. There are specifics points, some legal, regarding e-mail Do not do anything that would disrupt the use of others. Respect intellectual property of others by citing sources, and respect copyright laws relating to downloading text and software.

   No Warranties. This is a legal-sounding phrase that means the school district will not be responsible for lost data or services.

   Security. Never try to log on as another person. Never try to log on as a system operator. If we decide you are a security risk for any of our systems (Internet, Library Network, or computer lab), your privileges will be revoked.

   Vandalism. Vandalism includes any attempt to harm or destroy hardware, software, or data of another user. This would include uploading or creating computer viruses or breaching security measures.

GUIDED PRACTICE

Consider and discuss possible situations/scenarios (what-ifs).

INDEPENDENT PRACTICE

Students read and sign an Internet use agreement. Students take the document home for parents or guardians to read and sign. Students return the signed form to the library media center.

To use the transparency for this lesson on CD-ROM:

1. Open the CD-ROM and go to the Chapter 26 Folder.
2. Click to open the Folder.
3. Scroll to Acceptable Use document.
4. Click to open.

Acceptable Internet Use

Acceptable Use

Privileges

Netiquette

No Warranties

Security

Vandalism

PART IV:
ADDITIONAL INSTRUCTIONAL RESOURCES FOR USE THROUGHOUT THE YEAR

27 PRESEARCH FORMS AND PATHFINDERS

Careful attention to presearching activities results in more successful research projects. The following forms are intended to help plan and conduct searches.

To use the sample forms described in this section on CD-ROM:

1. Open the CD-ROM and go to the Chapter 27 Folder.
2. Click to open the Folder.
3. Scroll to the form you wish to use.
4. Click to open.

Library Catalog Presearch Planning Sheet

I am curious about _____

One thing I want to know about is _____

_____

Library Catalog Presearch Planning Sheet

I am curious about _____

One thing I want to know about is _____

_____

Search Strategy Worksheet

1. What is the problem you need to know more about? Write it in one sentence:

   _____

2. Brainstorm **key word(s),** the most important words, ideas, or phrases, from the sentence above. Use these key words to do your research.

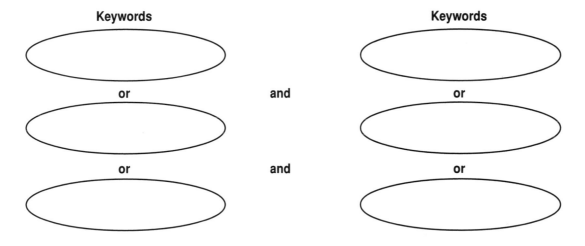

Keywords

or

and

Keywords

or

or

and

or

Search Statement:

_____

3. List other usable keywords. Consider synonyms, related terms, phrases, spellings, plurals or singulars, proper nouns, and truncation.

4. Which type of source listed below do you think will be the most useful? Number it "1". Place a "2" for your second choice and a "3" for the third best place to look.

   ____ Reference Collection   ____ Newspapers

   ____ Book Collection   ____ Personal interviews

   ____ Magazines   ____ Other "outside" resources (local libries, agencies, Internet)

5. What worked well? What should you try differently next time?

Secondary Research Guide

Name _____ **Teacher/Period**_____ / _____

Define the Problem   Describe your research topic. What particular aspect or point of view will you include?

1. Brainstorm possible **key words** (consider related terms).

Specific:		General:	

2. Consider which key words may be more helpful if **truncated**. List, showing the truncated form, e.g., teen* for teen, teenager, teens, etc.

3. Consider how key words could be linked with **Boolean connectors**. Compose several **search statements** using key words and Boolean connectors.

_____

_____

_____

_____

Sample Elementary Pathfinder

The following sources may be used when locating materials in the media center.

General Collection: Browse or use the library catalog using a key-word search. The call number listed on the screen will indicate the address of each material on the library shelf.

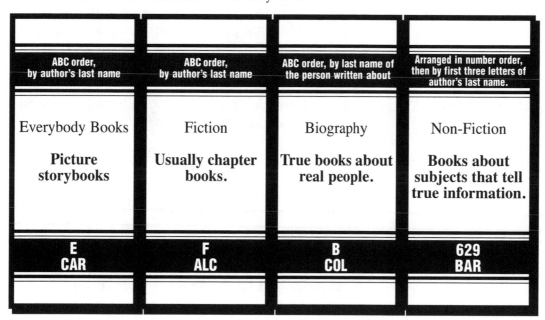

ABC order, by author's last name	ABC order, by author's last name	ABC order, by last name of the person written about	Arranged in number order, then by first three letters of author's last name.
Everybody Books **Picture storybooks**	Fiction **Usually chapter books.**	Biography **True books about real people.**	Non-Fiction **Books about subjects that tell true information.**
E CAR	F ALC	B COL	629 BAR

Reference Collection: Use these books to look up answers to your questions. Usually people do not read these cover to cover or take them from the media center.

_____ Encyclopedias: Articles about people, places, things (ABC order)
World Book, The New Book of Knowledge, The New Grolier Encyclopedia (print)
Encarta, First Connections, Information Finder, Groliers (CD-ROM)

_____ Almanacs: Includes all type of records–statistics, charts, tables, addresses
World Almanac, Information Please.

_____ Atlases: Maps, charts, tables of information about regions and countries of the world.

_____ Biographical dictionaries: Contributions and information about real people.

_____ Geographical Dictionaries: Descriptions of locations all over the world

_____ Special sources: Information on one subject.
Mammals, The Animals. The Way Things Work, America Alive, Dinosaurs (CD-ROMs), *Guiness Book of Records.*

Magazines: Use these to read stories or research about science, wildlife, hobbies, history, sports.
National Geographic World, Ranger Rick, Cobblestone, Faces, Sports Illustrated for Kids, American Girl, Scienceland, Spider, Ladybug, Cricket.

Community Members: Interview people to gain expert information, e.g., family members, students, teachers, people in our community.

Outside Sources: Use the computer to connect with the public library or to the Internet.

Sample General Pathfinder–Secondary

General Pathfinder

Reference Collection................ Includes many general and specialized reference tools. Most are print versions, but we have a growing number of CD-ROM tools as well. Check these out at the circulation desk.

General Collection .... Use electronic library catalog to locate print and nonprint resources in the collection.

Magazines..................................... Use *Magazine Article Summaries* (*MAS*) on the library network to locate magazine articles. Magazines are available for one-day checkout at the circulation desk. Some magazines are available on microfilm.

Newspapers................................ Use *NewsBank* on the library network to locate newspaper articles. The full-text articles may be printed out.

SIRS.. Use the *SIRS* Index on the library network to locate *SIRS* article reprints. The articles are in binders behind the circ desk and are available for 1-day checkout.

World Wide Web......................... Use AltaVista or another search engine on the Internet to access a wide range of information. Internet is accessible on any library network workstation.

Knowledgeable
Individuals .... Arrange a time to interview an "expert" on your topic. Be prepared with questions to ask and to take notes.

Outside Sources........................ Telnet from any library network workstation to the public library catalog or the university library catalog.

Questions?
Please ask for assistance. We are here to help!

28 ELEMENTARY AND SECONDARY BIBLIOGRAPHIC AIDS

Teachers may require students to keep a log or "working bibliography" form as they search and find information in various sources. The following samples can be used by students to record their sources and take notes on the information they find. Working Bibliography 1 is a simpler version and can be used to introduce the concept. It includes forms for book and encyclopedia entries *only*. Working Bibliography 2 and 3 forms include additional information options and can be used if a teacher wishes the students to complete a more formal bibliography.

While elementary students are not expected to master bibliographic format and rules regarding citation, they should be aware of issues related to plagiarism and copyright. Learning to give credit for information or to cite resources is an important part of any research project. Information copied word for word must always be cited as should major ideas and concepts that are not the student's own. At a very early level, students can be taught to cite a source by using parentheses right after the sentence that gives the information learned. It could be a person's name or the author and page number of a resource book:

"A long time ago in Iowa children used to walk to school in all kinds of weather. There were not any school buses" (My grandma).

"Dogs sweat through their tongues. It is the way they get rid of extra heat in their bodies (Allen, 34).

"John F. Kennedy said, 'Ask not what your country can do for you, ask what you can do for your country'" (*World Book*).

For further information see

1. Kemper, Dave, Verne Meyer, and Patrick Sebranek. *Write Source 2000: A Guide to Writing, Thinking & Learning*. Burlington, Wis.: Write Source Educational Publishing House, 1992.
2. Kemper, Dave, Ruth Nathan, and Patrick Sebranek. *Writer's Express: A Handbook for Young Writers, Thinkers, Learners*. Burlington, Wis.: Write Source Educational Publishing House, 1994.
3. Secondary bibliographic style sheet.

Working Bibliography 1

BOOK

Author_____
(last name)   (first name)

Title_____

What I learned:

_____

_____

_____

_____

ENCYCLOPEDIA

Subject heading _____

Encyclopedia _____

Pages _____

What I learned:

_____

_____

_____

_____

_____

Working Bibliography 2

BOOK

Author _____
            (last name)   (first name)

Title_____

Place of Publication_____

Publisher_____

Copyright date_____

Notes:

_____

_____

_____

_____

_____

_____

_____

_____

_____

_____

_____

_____

_____

_____

ENCYCLOPEDIA

Author (if found)_____

              (last name)   (first name)

Subject heading_____

Encyclopedia_____

Pages_____

Copyright Date_____

Volume_____

Notes

_____

_____

_____

_____

_____

_____

_____

_____

_____

_____

_____

_____

_____

Working Bibliography 3

SOURCE USED: _____

Format (videotape, CD-ROM, poster, pamphlet, personal interview, etc.)

_____

Author _____
          (last name)   (first)

Place of Publication _____

Publisher _____

Copyright Date _____

Notes

_____

_____

_____

_____

_____

_____

_____

_____

_____

_____

_____

_____

_____

_____

Research Log

Am pleased with the information I located and have printed out a bibliography or the text pertaining to my topic.	Found information using this source but could have found more precise information.	Thought this may be a helpful source but was unable to locate what I was searching for.	Didn't use this source.	**Resource**
				Reference Collection • includes general and specialized encyclopedias, dictionaries, statistical sources, etc., in print and electronic forms
				General Collection • use library catalog
				Magazines • use *MAS* on InfoNet • indexes 400 periodicals • updated monthly
				Newspapers • use *Newsbank* on InfoNet • full text • updated monthly
				SIRS • use *SIRS* on library network • full text • updated twice a year • includes graphs and tables
				WWW • launch Netscape • remember to record names and addresses of appropriate Web sites
				Knowledgeable individuals
				Outside sources • consider other libraries such as other schools in the district (on InfoNet), local public libraries, or the university • consider agencies or organizations

Standard Bibliography Style Sheet – Elementary

Book
O'Brien, J.B. *Surfing in Hawaii.* New York: Marine Press, 1995.

Encyclopedia Article – Author Not Given
"Bats." *World Book Encyclopedia.* 1997.

Encyclopedia Article – Author Given
Dana, Vernon. "The American Space Program." *Merit Students' Encyclopedia.* 1996.

CD ROM Encyclopedia
"TV Sets." *The Way Things Work.* CD-ROM. Dorling Kindersley, 1994.

Internet Article
"Pat Cummings." *Simon and Schuster Homepage.* Online. Internet. 26 Jan. 1998.

Magazine Article
Stein, Bart. "Caught in the World Wide Web." *National Geographic World.* June 1997: 24-25.

- Either underlining or italics are acceptable ways to indicate a title, although italics are preferred in word-processed documents.

- If a book or other material does not have an author, use the title or shortened form of the title in place of the author's last name. One-page articles and encyclopedia articles do not need page numbers.

- If you wish to use formal bibliographic format, you may wish to list sources on a separate page with the heading "Bibliography."

Standard Bibliographic Style Sheet – Secondary

BOOK WITH ONE AUTHOR
Gore, Al. *Earth in the Balance; Ecology and the Human Spirit.* Boston: Houghton Mifflin, 1992.

BOOK WITH TWO AUTHORS
Edey, Maitland A. and Donald C. Johanson. *Blueprints; Solving the Mystery of Evolution.* Boston: Little, Brown, 1989.

BOOK WITH A CORPORATE AUTHOR
Time-Life, Inc. *This Fabulous Century: 1950-1960.* New York: Time, Inc., 1970.

BOOK WITH AN EDITOR
Easter, Eric, D. Michael Cheers and Dudley M. Brooks, eds. *Songs of My People.* Boston: Little, Brown, 1992.

MAGAZINE ARTICLE–AUTHOR KNOWN
Church, George J. "Flood, Sweat and Tears." *Time* 26 July 1993: 22-33.

MAGAZINE ARTICLE–AUTHOR UNKNOWN
"Two Cheers for Demokratiya." *U.S. News & World Report* 5 Apr. 1993: 42-46.

NEWSPAPER ARTICLE–AUTHOR KNOWN
Smith, Donald. "Global Telecommuters Work from All Over." *Cedar Rapids Gazette* 25 Jul. 1993: C1+.

NEWSBANK ARTICLE
DiBacco, Thomas V. "Tracing the Trail of Alzheimers." *Washington Post* 29 Nov. 94: Z9. CD-ROM. *NewsBank,* 1994.

SIRS ARTICLE (FROM FULL-TEXT *SIRS RESEARCHER*)
Wartik, Nancy. "Tough Calls." *American Health* Mar. 1992: 58-62. CD-ROM. *SIRS Researcher,* 1996.

DICTIONARY ENTRY
"Populist." *Merriam-Webster's Collegiate Dictionary.* 10th ed. 1993.

ALMANAC ENTRY
"Chile." *The World Almanac Book of Facts.* 1994 ed.

ENCYCLOPEDIA ENTRY
Diehl, Paul B. "Poetry." *World Book Encyclopedia.* 1997 ed.

SPECIALIZED REFERENCE BOOK ENTRY
"Ginsburg, Ruth Bader." *Current Biography Yearbook.* 1994 ed.

INTERVIEW
Waller, Robert. Telephone interview. 20 Feb. 1993.

ARTICLE OR ESSAY IN COLLECTION
Chaucer, Geoffrey. "The Miller's Tale," *The Canterbury Tales,* trans. David Wright. New York: Oxford University Press, 1985.
Caldwell, Bettye. "The Condition of America's Poor Is Improving." *Poverty.* Opposing Viewpoints Series. San Diego: Greenhaven Press, 1994.

NONPRINT SOURCE
Lorraine Hansberry: The Black Experience in the Creation of Drama. Videocassette. Films for the Humanities and Sciences, 1992.

CD-ROM
"Brontë, Emily." *Discovering Authors.* CD-ROM. Detroit: Gale, 1992.
Fairbridge, Rhodes W. "Plate Tectonics." *Encarta.* CD-ROM. 1994 ed.

INFORMATION ACCESSED THROUGH A COMPUTER SERVICE (E.G., AMERICA ONLINE)
"Middle Ages." *Academic American Encyclopedia.* Online. America Online. 15 Oct. 1995.

INFORMATION ACCESSED THROUGH INTERNET
Willett, Edward F. "How Our Laws Are Made." *Thomas: Legislative Information on the Internet.* Online. Internet. 1 Nov. 1995. Available: http://www.thomas.loc.gov
Williamson, Jay. *Guns and the Constitution.* Online. Internet. 20 Nov. 1995. Available: http://www.vyne. comn/glow/guncntl/guncntl.html
"Crimes and Crime Rates, by Type." *Census Bureau Home Page.* Online. Internet. 27 Nov. 1995. Available: http://www.census.gov/

GENERAL TIPS

- If you use a source not listed here, consult the *MLA Handbook for Writers of Research Papers* (Ref 808.02 Gib) or ask a librarian for assistance or consult
- If you cannot find a date, use the abbreviation n.d. (no date). If you cannot find a page, use n.p. (no page).
- Entries are in alphabetical order.
- The first line of each entry begins at the left margin. The second line (if needed) is indented five spaces.
- Single-space within an entry. Double space between entries.
- Underlining may be used rather than italics, if the document is not being word processed or the teacher prefers underlining.
- Do not label the entries with the type of source (e.g. Magazine).
- The following is an example of what a completed bibliography should look like.

Bibliography

"Brontë, Emily." *Discovering Authors*. CD-ROM. Detroit: Gale, 1992.

Caldwell, Bettye. "The Condition of America's Poor Is Improving." *Poverty*. Opposing Viewpoints Series. San Diego: Greenhaven Press, 1994.

"Chile." *The World Almanac Book of Facts*. 1994 ed.

Church, George J. "Flood, Sweat and Tears." *Time* 26 Jul. 1993: 22-33.

DiBacco, Thomas V. "Tracing the Trail of Alzheimers." *Washington Post* 29 Nov. 94: Z9. CD-ROM. *NewsBank*, 1994.

Diehl, Paul B. "Poetry." *World Book Encyclopedia*. 1997 ed.

Edey, Maitland A. and Donald C. Johanson. *Blueprints; Solving the Mystery of Evolution*. Boston: Little, Brown, 1989.

Fairbridge, Rhodes W. "Plate Tectonics." *Encarta*. CD-ROM. 1994 ed.

"Ginsburg, Ruth Bader." *Current Biography Yearbook*. 1994 ed.

"Middle Ages." *Academic American Encyclopedia*. Online. America Online. 15 Oct. 1995.

"Populist." *Merriam-Webster's Collegiate Dictionary*. 10th ed. 1993.

Smith, Donald. "Global Telecommuters Work from All Over." *Cedar Rapids Gazette* 25 Jul. 1993: C1+.

Time-Life, Inc. *This Fabulous Century: 1950-1960*. New York: Time, Inc., 1970.

"Two Cheers for Demokratiya." *U.S. News & World Report* 5 Apr. 1993: 42-46.

Waller, Robert. Telephone interview. 20 Feb. 1993.

Wartik, Nancy. "Tough Calls." *American Health* Mar. 1992: 58-62. CD-ROM. *SIRS Researcher*, 1996.

Willett, Edward F. "How Our Laws Are Made." *Thomas: Legislative Information on the Internet*. Online. Internet. 1 Nov. 1995. Available: http://www.thomas.loc.gov

29 THE SCHOOL LIBRARY MEDIA CENTER'S WEB SITE

A useful tool for students and staff as they use the Internet is a library Web site that provides ready access to commonly used reference sources and other online tools. Such a Web site, designed by the library media specialist, serves to improve the efficiency of those who are using the Web by organizing information for quick access—a traditional library role! The example of such a Web site shown is from the Iowa City Community School District. The high school media specialist who designed this site chose three major areas of emphasis—*Newspapers*, because students and staff are frequently searching for newspaper articles or simply wanting to read newspapers online; *Government*, because classes do a research assignment three times per year that requires use of these common government sources, and *References*, with links to a variety of frequently used reference tools, including the online MLA Formatting Guide for easy access when students have questions about bibliographic format. Reference also includes sources frequently used in the various curricular areas.

The sampling of links from the library Web page shown illustrates the usefulness of such a page. A number of these are sources of local interest that you would want to tailor to your specific needs. To view the entire page online, use the URL http://www.iowa-city.k12.ia.us/Schools/City/lib.html.

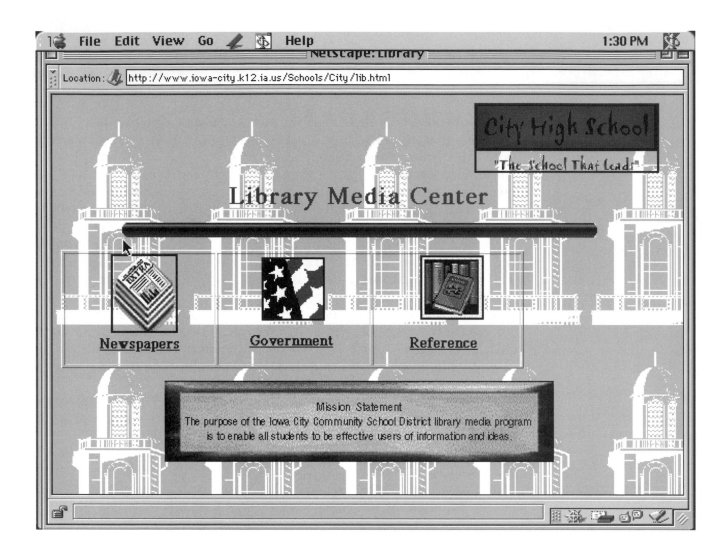

SAMPLE LINKS FROM CITY HIGH SCHOOL WEB PAGE

Newspapers	Government	Reference
Local Little Hawk (school paper) The Cedar Rapids Gazette The Des Moines Register Collection *United States* Boston Globe Online The Chicago Tribune USA Today The New York Times The Wall Street Journal *International* The Times of London The Sydney Morning Herald LeMonde...*from France* El Pais...*from Spain*	*National Government* Library of Congress Homepage The White House Thomas Legislative Information from the US Congress The Smithsonian Institution *State Government* The State of Iowa Homepage Iowa Official Register Code of Iowa *Other Sites* Stately Knowledge	*General Reference* Encarta Online Bartlett, John, Familiar Quotations Internet Public Library Ready Reference Collection MLA Format: Giving Credit to Sources Research It! *Art* Web Museum Famous Paintings World Arts Resources *Economics* Stock Master AMEX Stock Exchange NASDAQ *Foreign Language* Online Dictionaries and Translators

INDEX

ABOUT THE DEVELOPERS OF THE INFORMATION LITERACY PROGRAM

The Iowa City Community School District received the School Library Media Program of the Year Award in 1997. The curriculum review process, which resulted in this guide, along with strong administrative support and excellent staff were cited as strengths of the program in the award description. The district includes 22 school buildings for grades K-12.

Nearly all district media specialists were involved in the development of this guide and are listed below.

Mary Jo Langhorne
Media Coordinator

Barbara Becker
Lucas Elementary School

Elizabeth Belding
West High School

Suzanne Bork
Kirkwood Elementary School

Patricia Braunger
Wood Elementary School

Susan Corbin-Muir
Hills Elementary School

Becky Gelman
Coralville Central Elementary School

Ann Holton
Penn Elementary School

Anne Marie Kraus
Roosevelt Elementary School

Mary MacNeil
Shimek Elementary School

Dolores Madden
Hoover Elementary School

Deborah McAlister
City High School

Lynn Myers
Twain Elementary School

Karen Parker
Longfellow Elementary School

Lisa Petrie
City High School

Denise Rehmke
West High School.

Susan Richards
Northwest Junior High School

Cathy Schiele
Horn Elementary School

Joel Shoemaker
South East Junior High School

Barbara Stein
Weber Elementary School

Victoria Walton
Mann Elementary School

Nancy Weber
Lincoln Elementary School

Nancy Westlake
Lemme Elementary School